My Dishwasher Theology

My Dishwasher Theology

Thinking about the Big Questions
of Christian Faith

André M. Stephany

RESOURCE *Publications* · Eugene, Oregon

MY DISHWASHER THEOLOGY
Thinking about the Big Questions of Christian Faith

Resource Publications
An Imprint of Wipf and Stock Publishers
199 W. 8th Ave., Suite 3
Eugene, OR 97401

www.wipfandstock.com

PAPERBACK ISBN: 978-1-6667-0451-8
HARDCOVER ISBN: 978-1-6667-0452-5
EBOOK ISBN: 978-1-6667-0453-2

JUNE 14, 2021

+

In the Name of God, Father, Son, and Holy Spirit.

Soli Deo Gloria

In gratefulness to my parents, Bernd and Martina.

Contents

Acknowledgements

WHEN I WROTE THIS book, I was guest on the ancestral and unceded territories of the Coast Salish Peoples: the Musqueam, Squamish, and Tsleil-Waututh nations. I am grateful for the hospitality I enjoy as an uninvited guest.

I want to give thanks to the wonderful Amer Aiyub, without whose encouragement I would not have written this text and, especially, would not have finished it in good spirit. There are so many people who deserve thanks and I will just name a few as representatives for the many others to whom I am grateful. There are teachers who have formed me in my theology and preaching like The Rev'd Dr. Dieter Splinter, The Rev'd Dr. Caroline Schroeder Field, The Rev'd Philipp Roth (who does not like the title Rev'd) and theological super heroes who have influenced me greatly like Karl Barth, Jürgen Moltmann, Martin Luther.

And there are the wonderful people who agreed to do the very tiring task of proof-reading. A big Thank You to our dear friend Bill Orr who endured the tiring task to correct a German's English without any complaining and in his typical humility and gentleness. Thanks to the support and encouragement of dear friends as The Rev'd Dr. Stuart Mennigke, June Wright, and others.

And a big thank you to the anonymous inventor of the title of this book. I heard this title during my training in the Swiss Reformed Church and am very grateful for the idea. I hope that I have used it for a good purpose.

List of Abbreviations

Gen	Genesis
Deut	Deuteronomy
Ps	Psalm
Isa	Prophet Isaiah
Matt	Gospel of Matthew
Mark	Gospel of Mark
Luke	Gospel of Luke
Acts	Acts of the Apostles
Rom	Letter to the Romans
1 Cor	First Letter to the Corinthians
1 Thess	First Letter to the Thessalonians
1 John	First Letter of John
Rev	Revelation
NRSV	New Revised Standard Version
WA	Weimarer Ausgabe
WA DB	Weimarer Ausgabe Deutsche Bibel
BC	Before Christ
AD	Anno Domini

LGBTQI2 Acronymn for Lesbian, Gay, Bisexual, Transgender, Queer, Intersex, Asexual, Two-Spirit, and the countless affirmative ways in which people choose to self-identify

I

Introduction

"My Dishwasher Theology": what is that supposed to mean? If you were hoping for a theology around the noble act of dishwashing, I have to disappoint you. The theology discussed in this small book is Christian theology and the questions are some of the core questions of Christian faith. The reason for the title? If you are a believer, you might have had this experience; definitely every theology student or minister has had it: you are washing the dishes with people and chatting about the delicious cake, when suddenly someone turns to you and says: "You are a believer/theologian/ priest. You can definitely answer my question." What follows is usually a very complex and fundamental question of faith, such as: "My husband died last year. Where do you think is he now?" Or: "My granddaughter will be baptized. What happens in Baptism?"

These situations are the nightmare of many early students in seminaries and theological faculties and just to think of such a moment can make them tremble (I felt like that). The thing with these questions is that, yes, they are actually very basic and people just assume that every believer or at least every first semester theologian learns *the* answer to them. But these questions are the kind of hard nuts which none of us can ever crack fully and for which you need years of spiritual and academic experience, a lot of prayer and frustration, before you find temporary answers which work for you. At the same time, such moments are wonderful opportunities to share core believes and for the person asking, the question is often existential. Just to say, "Oh, I am going to have a lecture about this question next semester," does not lead to a satisfying conversation. This small book is my response to a number of such questions. The intention is not to give answers, especially not the answer. What I tried to do in writing it is to take you by the hand and to look at landmarks along the path that leads me to my very personal answer. I hope this book can be a help for you to think, meditate, pray, listen, and to develop your own Dishwasher Theology. The answers I give are my personal answers right now, at this moment when I write. I am fully aware that they will develop and change; maybe tomorrow, I will answer some of the questions differently. Theology flows out of a living relationship with God and in a relationship, nothing is static. Yes, God is the same from age to age but God is so much more than we can understand and no human being has ever seen God in completeness, except for Jesus. That means that a relationship with God will always bring new understanding, new insights, and surprises.

What theological background can you expect? It makes me a bit sad that today's theological landscape, allegedly, is so easily divided into conservative and liberal. Conservative—in this binary thinking—means a more literal understanding of the Bible, often more conservative in questions of society: anti-LGBTQI2+, arguing about the full equality of women. Liberal means that you treat the Bible as a historical document which has to be read with the tools you would use to read such a document from a different period. Many Liberals are considered less Christ-centered or see Jesus rather as a good man, a prophet, than as the Son of God.

It often surprises me how many theologians would accept this over-simplification of the theological landscape that thinks so much in boxes. I want to be conservative and liberal! I want to be a liberal conservative. For me, the Bible is inspired by the Holy Spirit, while written by humans. God can speak through the Bible and there is no question that the Bible is our highest source of Divine Revelation. The same is true for Christ. Christ has to be head, heart, and center of the church and Christ died, rose from the dead and ascended into heaven. For me, there is no way to change something around these core beliefs without altering the whole belief-system.

At the same time, I believe in a loving God who gave us the Bible as Good News and not as a summary of all the people who are condemned. I am liberal because I believe that God's creation is good in its variety and beauty and that we all have the same standing before God. I am liberal because I do not see my task as a Christian to tell others that they do not believe in the right way, but trust that God uses people of all faiths and of none to shape this world in preparation of the Kingdom.

I invite us all to reject the easy line between conservative and liberal. With this little book, I try to model what I mean by a liberal conservative theology. Difficult texts from the Bible cannot just be put aside. They are part of our tradition and at a minimum we need to honor them by wrestling with them. A strong faith can wrestle with holy texts and even with God. When I do that, I always ask myself: where is the call to action in this text, where is the Good News, where is the historical and contextual part? Where does God speak, where do humans speak and I ask you: where do you hear God speak to you and what does God say?

I am an Anglican Priest with a German and Swiss Protestant background and training which have definitely influenced my theology. My spirituality is strongly centered on the Eucharist and I have an Anglo-Catholic leaning in my sacramental theology. There are references to the Anglican tradition throughout this book and I took the freedom to use the inclusive pronouns *us* and *we* taking the reader into the Christian family. I hope you will not experience that as intrusive, for it is not meant to be.

At this point, I want to acknowledge gratefully that the title of this book is not my own invention. I learned about the expression in German during my training in the Swiss Reformed Church and copy it here into English with gratefulness for the creativity of its original inventor.

The Bible translations used in this book are either my own (marked with AS) or taken from the New Revised Standard Version (NRSV, every time when not marked).

God is not an old man with a beard as God is so often depicted. As much as possible, I have tried to avoid pronouns but there are still many of them left. I tried to vary between she/her and he/him/his.

II

Do you believe in the Bible?

OR: THE ROLE OF SCRIPTURE

MOST PEOPLE WHO HAVE outed themselves as Christians have encountered this question at one point of their journey. "Do you believe in the Bible?" Neither a quick *yes* nor a general *no* will really answer this question for most Christians. If you dare the endeavor of giving a more diversified and more complex answer, you will quickly realize that this is not what your counterpart was looking for. However, if we want to honor the Bible, we should be brave and remain true to ourselves.

As Christians, we do not believe *in* the Bible, we believe in God. We believe that the Bible is a collection of holy texts, books actually, that reveal God's history with humankind and God's interaction with creation throughout history from a human perspective. The Bible can best be described as a library. What is so easily treated as one book, is in reality a collection of books, originally scrolls for the most part. There are a number of ways to group them. We commonly divide them by the two categories of Old Testament and New Testament. Many prefer to call them First and Second Testament or Hebrew Bible and New Testament. Old and new sound like one was the old-fashioned one and the new was the up-date; which is definitely not the understanding. The Hebrew Bible and its books are the roots of Christianity. We share it with Judaism. Jesus, who was a Jew for all of his life, grew up with these texts. His spirituality and his ritual were shaped by the Hebrew Bible and Jewish practices. Most of the first Christians were Jewish, some of the authors of the New Testament as well—just think of Paul. The world, the thoughts, the ways in which Jesus and the first Christians acted cannot be understood without understanding the Hebrew Scriptures and the challenges of Judaism under Roman occupation.

The Hebrew Bible is in itself subdivided into different categories. There are the five so called Books of Moses, the Historical Books, the Prophets, the Psalms and more. They are all completely different in style. However, what unites them all is that humans wrote down their experience with God in a certain situation. The Scriptures themselves never claim to be written or dictated by God (except the Ten Commandments). They were all written by *normal* people who tried to make sense of their time and who tried to pass on how they experienced God at work in their life. The authors used different ways of doing this. For the story of Creation, the authors wanted to express their strong believe that God is in all, that God is the gracious God who has created this world and enabled life, that God created order by making an end to chaos.

In the story of Creation, God is introduced to us as the One source of all being. God is also introduced as the faithful companion of the Israelites. Every time they break God's commandments, kill each other, deceive each other or violate God's creation, God remains faithful.

The story of Creation or—here comes the point—rather the stories of Creation never intended to give us a detailed account of Creation. It is a mystery how people could and seriously still can put scientific discoveries about the coming into existence of the world and the biblical narrative into contradiction. The Hebrew Bible itself did not mind putting two different narratives just next to each other: Genesis 1 with the six days of Creation and the Sabbath and then Genesis 2 that gives us another account. It was never about the detailed report; it has always been about God's role, God's love immanent in her Creation. God all in all, God the faithful, God who brings order.

If you want to take the Bible seriously, then do not assume its authors were ignorants who did not realize what they were doing by giving us two different accounts which cannot be unified or by telling us that Adam and Eve, and their kids Cain and Abel were the only humans on earth while suddenly their children got married to other humans (Gen 4:17). Eden is not equivalent to the whole earth; it is the beginning of God's special relationship with one people.

Do you believe *in* the Bible? What is meant is: do you believe in a story like this literally? The great revelation is that many Bible stories do not want to be understood literally but trust their readers to see the message behind and to see through the veil of the actual narrative. This depends on the biblical books. If you have more historical accounts like in the Books of Kings, the idea of the authors is a different one than in allegorical stories like Creation or the Book of Jonah.

The authors of the Bible were faithful people who tried to make sense of the times they lived in and to find God in all of their experiences. If you lived in a peaceful time where civilization around you blossomed, you would write hymns of praise and thanksgiving and write about God as peace bringer and preserver. If you lived in times of war, you had to make sense of the brutality, the failure of human morals, suffering, and death. Where was/is God in this? Some authors gave the (debatable) answer: war was punishment for disobedience or luck in war was a reward for obedience. It is easy to blame the writers to see God as an angry, brutal God who launches war and sends thousands to death but if you lived in a time of constant massacre and you believe that God is a powerful God, then this is one possible conclusion. Our image of the angry God as God of the Old Testament and the Loving God of the New Testament comes from there. This image is not right and is just the result of a superficial involvement with the Hebrew Scriptures. To blame an *angry God* for war or—worse—blame the

Jewish God, is the result of an actual speechlessness when confronted with the question: where is God in the suffering of this World and how can God allow suffering? Every believer must wrestle with this question, probably a lifelong, and every believer must retain from giving an easy answer.

While the question around the existence of evil in God's world (Theodicy) will play a role in this book later, just as much here: my reply (at the moment and it is developing, changing and evolving constantly) is inspired by Jürgen Moltmann's concept of the God Crucified. Where is God in the suffering? Right in the midst of it. Where is God in war? Right in the trenches, beside the dying, next to the dying child, behind the grieving mother . . . God's real power is not the power of weapons and armies; it is the power of love and of faithfulness even in the darkest hours.

Moving to the New Testament, the things already mentioned apply. In the New Testament, we find four accounts of Jesus's life, which are all a bit different, however, three of them are very much related to one another. We also find the Acts of the Apostles and a number of Letters from various early Christians, most prominent among them St. Paul.

Do you believe in the Bible? I do believe that Jesus healed people, not just in a spiritual sense. I do believe, Jesus performed miracles. Could he walk on water? Well, if God sees a benefit in him walking on water, sure. Did it necessarily happen exactly like we find it written? Maybe, but maybe not. Again, to honor the Scriptures is not necessarily to take everything literally.

There is this famous story of Jesus healing the blind man in Bethsaida told in the Gospel of Mark (Mark 8:22–26).

> Do I believe Jesus could and did heal blind people?
>
> Yes, I do.
>
> Has this story happened like laid down in the Gospel of Mark?
>
> Probably not.
>
> Why?
>
> This story is just too perfect.

Everything in this miracle is carefully placed. The healing happens right in the middle of the Gospel of Mark in chapter 8 (the Gospel of Mark has 16 chapters).[1] Jesus had just fed four thousand people with seven loaves of bread and a few small fish (Mark 8:1–9), when the Pharisees (a very pious religious group in ancient Judaism) demanded a sign (Mark 8:11). What Jesus had done before was not enough; they wanted more. Also, his disciples proved yet again that they still did not understand who Jesus was. He replied, "Having eyes, do you not see?" (Mark 8:18, AS). The healing of the blind man happened right after these two groups of religious people had questioned Jesus's authority and true being. The ones who should be trained to see signs of God when they happen, especially when they happen in front of their eyes, proved to be blind. Jesus healed the man but needed two attempts. First, his sight came back partially but then "his sight was restored, and he saw everything clearly" (Mark 8:25b). What a nice parallel to his disciples. They met Jesus and followed him because they had begun to see; not fully yet but vaguely. But then, after this healing of the blind man, Peter finally understood who Jesus really was. They go to a place called Caesarea Philippi, at the foot of Mount Hermon in the North of the Holy Land; a "pagan" city as the name gives away. Named in honor of *Caesar*, the Roman emperor Augustus by the local ruler Philip II (from King Herod the Great's family). In this city stood a huge temple for the God *Pan* (from the Greek word for *all/everything*), hence the God of All. In this city, Peter recognized who the real God of All is and who had been sent by him as his anointed: Jesus.

"You are the Messiah" (Mark 8:29b; *Messiah=the Anointed*). Right in the middle of the Gospel, Peter confesses Jesus as the Messiah. It is the turning point in the Gospel, the hinge. The healing of the blind man might have happened in one way or the other, but as it is described here follows too many rules for a nice literary arrangement. After the eyes were opened, Peter began to see and with him, the world began to see who Jesus really was.

1. Even though the verse and chapter numbers were inserted into the text much later, it is still the middle of the Gospel.

The author of the Gospel of Mark had a big number of written sayings and stories, anecdotes about Jesus in front of him, as well as many oral narratives. Mark's task was to arrange them in a way that made sense, that was worthy of Jesus the Messiah. For me, Mark did that masterfully.

> Now, is this story worth less, if it did not happen exactly in that way?
>
> Not at all.

I strongly believe that the authors of the Holy Scriptures were inspired by the Holy Spirit. They wanted to give their readers the best and, consequently, worthiest report of Jesus's life and they did it well. Jesus comes alive when we share these stories with each other, the spirit of Jesus's actions, his Godly authority, his healing power, all comes alive and present in sharing these stories for us as followers of Jesus.

To make it very clear, I do not believe all the stories in the Gospels have been made up. The authors of the Gospels based their story lines on written and oral accounts from eyewitnesses. It is just the question whether really every story has happened exactly as recorded. I see this way taking Scripture more seriously than the literal understanding. Else, what would you make of non-congruent stories? Was Jesus born in a stable or a house (Luke vs. Matthew), did his parents flee to Egypt or did they stay and present Jesus in the Temple and then go back to Nazareth? If you want to believe it all literally, then you have to come up with strange unifying theories, while you can let both accounts stand next to each other, believing that both authors built their story line on different sources that might all have a true core, just the exact sequence of events has gone lost. Now, were Mary and Joseph originally from Nazareth and did they go to Bethlehem only for the Roman registration where Jesus happened to be born, or were they originally from Bethlehem and the Roman registration did not play any role in the birth of Jesus? Or was Jesus even born in Nazareth? Does the answer to this really shake the foundations of our belief, knowing that both authors had other passages of Scripture and prophesies in mind, which they saw fulfilled?

There are also the letters, especially, the letters from St. Paul. Paul was a very interesting character and he left us strong testimonies of faith that can still encourage and lighten the fire of faith in our hearts. There is wisdom in his words, with stubbornness and an unparalleled love for the Good News and the proclamation of the Gospel of Jesus Christ. St. Paul has also left us some rather unhelpful pieces of advice on the role of women, human sexuality and disciplinary measures. What to do with them?

The authors of the New Testament were human beings living in their times, in their places, shaped by the culture and tradition of their time. We have to keep this in mind, when reading their moral outlines and regulations. If we had not done this before, we would as Christians also still tolerate slavery because it has a scriptural foundation. The Spirit is at work in the Bible but also in history and she is continually revealing God's plan for us. We have to embrace this development of unfolding love.

Having said this, it is important to emphasize: the Bible is not a buffet where we pick what we like and leave what we do not like. If we do not like something we have to wrestle with it, we have to pray about it, we must not dispel it easily. Martin Luther (1483–1546) had the wonderful image of the center of Scripture, a guiding thread through Scripture. For him the guiding thread was Jesus Christ (*Was Christum treibet*).[2] Jesus Christ and what he taught and lived was the center of Scripture and the measurement for every passage. Was a passage not compatible with the core teachings of Jesus, then, it was not in line with the guiding thread. He wrote this in his famous preamble for the Letter of James (*Jakobusbrief*) which he wanted to move to the end of the New Testament because he found it contradictory to core teachings of the Gospels and of Paul. This opinion is very debatable and today theologians are more careful with trying to impose Jesus Christ on

2. Luther, WA DB 7:384, 26–32. Translated, it means *What pushes Christ / What drives Christ.*

every text of the Hebrew Bible,[3] but the hermeneutical principle of the Golden or Guiding Thread (hermeneutical=a principle to interpret the Bible) is still very helpful.

For me, this guiding thread, the center of the whole Bible is God's unconditional love for his creation and for humans in particular. I do not mean this in a romantic kitschy way, with God just being love and everything is love and we love each other. I mean it in a demanding way, also, like a real relationship that demands work, mutual respect, obedience, sacrifices. Luther's idea was that every passage of Scripture has to be tested against this guiding thread, thrown against this main and leading principle like it was a rock. What crashed and broke at the stone was not worth to be considered in eternity, what survived was.

> Do you believe in the Bible?
>
> No, Christians do not believe *in* the Bible, they believe in God.
>
> What is the Bible then?

Among nearly all Christian Denominations, probably all, the Bible has the highest authority and is the prime source of legitimacy. It gets tricky when we ask whether the Bible is the only source of legitimacy. As Christians, we believe that God has revealed himself in the Bible. God has chosen the stories of the Bible to be the medium to speak to us, for us to learn about God and God's plans for us. Also in Jesus, God revealed himself and showed his true face, his true intentions towards humankind. The Bible is our prime source about Jesus Christ and, therefore, the source of God's self-revelation.

But is it the only source of revelation? Can you learn about God without or apart from the Bible? Can you make statements

---

3. Luther also said that Christians are the only ones who can understand the Old Testament fully and correctly because they know Jesus Christ who has been announced in the Old Testament and who brought the light and reason for scripture: „Wir Christen haben den synn und verstand der Biblia, weil wir das Newe Testament, das ist Jhesum Christum haben, welcher im alten Testament verheissen und hernach komen, mit sich das liecht und verstand der schrifft bracht hat, wie er spricht Joh. 5" (Luther, WA 54:29, 3–6).

about God, about God's laws, about Christian morality, etc. without the Bible or based on other sources of revelation, like nature for example? This has been a debate for many centuries. The answer of the Reformation was quite clear: the Bible is the only source of Revelation; every positive statement about God has to be proven by teachings of the Bible: *Sola Scriptura*, Martin Luther called this principle. *Scripture alone* is the source of our Christian understanding of God. This was an attempt to overcome the understanding of the church that while the Bible has the prime position among all sources of revelation and legitimation, tradition and human reason are also ways in which God has revealed himself to us.

All the great reformed theologians followed this principle loyally. Karl Barth (1886–1968), one of the most important theologians of the twentieth century, would even break the long friendship with his colleague Emil Brunner over the question whether humans had a natural instinct for God or not.[4] Has God revealed herself in nature as well (natural theology)? Can you get a sense of God, meet God, feel awe in the presence of God in nature without Holy Scriptures? While Barth would later develop his initial strong *No!* into a *no, but*, most of his life he would argue that you cannot have any idea of God, if not through Jesus Christ, the true Revelation of God. No comparison from an earthly entity or concept was appropriate for God, Barth argued. You cannot say, for example, God was like a father, because God is the one and only real father and we only understand what parenthood really means through God. So Barth, turned the direction around. It is not us who can explain God, try to compare God or find God, it is God who has chosen—in her absolute freedom—to reveal herself and to make herself known to us.

Nothing without the Bible, *Sola Scriptura*, would be this line of argument. Personally, I have a broader understanding of God's ways of self-revelation. The Bible is the highest source of authority and revelation but I believe that God has continually revealed herself in history and still reveals herself now. That is why, for me, the

4. Barth, *Nein! Antwort an Emil Brunner*,

traditions of the church, the way we have celebrated services, worshipped God, celebrated the Eucharist, why the many teachings of the theologians of the past centuries, why all this still matters. I also think that God has not given us reason in order not to use it but to apply this precious gift in order to grow in knowledge and love of God. Each age of time has its own challenges and questions. The Bible speaks into each age and to each generation but we need to apply reason and our developing experience in order to make appropriate and wise decisions.

Christians should not deal with Holy Scripture heedlessly. It is the duty of a Christian to wrestle with the Bible and especially the challenging texts and not to suspend them light-heartedly but prayer, reasoning and listening to God might convince you that not every verse of this sacred text gives the right directive for every situation in every age.

God has indeed chosen to reveal himself in Jesus Christ, to become human, and also to allow that believers recorded God's self-revelation in the books of the Bible. I am sure God knew that this would lead to a multitude of interpretations; so we should not be afraid of disagreement.

If God created the world, I also strongly believe that you find the creator in nature and in every creature, especially in every human being. This means that, although, the Bible is the prime source of self-revelation, God can be encountered and always has been in nature, history, and especially in the other. This is not a free pass to make up your own God as you would like. At the end of the day, we have to measure our experiences of God, the Divine against the Bible, the center of the Bible to remind us of Luther again.

Do you believe in the Bible?

No, I do not believe *in* the Bible. I believe in God.

However, the Bible is a wonderful and sacred collection of stories written by people who have experienced God's presence in their life. Many of these stories help me to understand God better and to see how he loves us; so much that God became one of us himself.

III

Are not all Religions the Same?

OR: GOD

WHAT USUALLY IS BEHIND this question is an interest in learning more about God, God's existence, and the differences between the way Christians and believers from other religions see God. Are they not all the same? You would encounter this question either in regard to other religions or even in a context where someone is thinking of siblings of another Christian denomination. While the answer to Christian siblings is clearly a *yes*, let us have a closer look at this question. I can already admit that I do believe that there is only one God and I also believe that the three religions of the Books (Judaism, Christianity, Islam) worship the same God but the differences in understanding this God are quite considerable and the answer *yes, they are* should not be made without knowing about these differences, or at least the Christian point of view.

Does God exist?

This is a question all religions have to answer and among the monotheistic (believing in one God) religions, the answer will be similar. Medieval theologians have tried to prove the existence of

God by logical deduction. Anselm of Canterbury (around 1033–1109) tried to give an *ontological* proof[1] (ontological=existing/being) and applied a very legalistic concept based on the necessity of salvation by God becoming human (*Cur Deus Homo*=Why became God human?), while Thomas Aquinas (1225–1274) took up the philosophical concept of the *Unmoved Mover* by Aristotle and thought God as the *First Cause*.

These concepts from both theologians are really interesting and enlightening; however, they do a very bad job in what they had set out to do: to prove the existence of God. The problem lies in the idea that God could be proven, or also the opposite: the non-existence of God could be proven. In order to prove something, you do not really need to understand it fully, however, in order to prove something, you need to be able to grasp something, get hold of something, make something visible to all. Here we have to return to Karl Barth: God's revelation happens only by grace and God's own decision. Nothing and no-one can force God to reveal himself. It is pure freedom when, where and to whom God reveals his loving presence.

This leaves those who try to defend God's existence against the doubts of critics in a weak position. It can be that just by what are considered rational arguments, the critics are likely to score. One of my professors once tried to describe this situation with an example. He said, if you had asked Mother Teresa when she was still alive, to sit on a stage and discuss with a scholarly critic, the debate about the probability of God's existence would very likely have been won by the scholar but would not just the presence of a saint like Mother Teresa and her life story which she represents in that moment, would not just her presence and the love in her eyes, the deep trust in God which you could just read from her eyes, would not that be the greatest proof of the existence of a loving power much greater and much more powerful than anything the human intellect could possibly understand and grasp?

---

1. Anselm, "Why God became Man?" 260–356; Anselm, *Opera omnia*, 89–139.

That is the main role saints play for me. They are not heroes from a different star, unreachable in their moral lives, but they are role-models for me and that not because they were perfect. They are role models because they managed at one point in their lives to trust God and live and die in trust. If we as humans experience God, become aware of God in our lives, or entrust ourselves to God, we need other examples. We need to know that we are not alone on this journey of growing into a relationship with God. The saints, or already the Apostles in the Bible can help us not only to see how faithful they were, but also that you do not *have* God after a certain experience. Peter, for example, just seconds after the moment when he had understood that Jesus was the Messiah—what a special spiritual moment—he was told off by Jesus for being too concerned with earthly things (Mark 8). God is a partner in a relationship, the moment you try to hold tight and take away the freedom of this partner, God disappears, withdraws. A relationship with God is a lifelong process of growing that also includes long periods of silence between the partners. The Bible has a number of passages that call to God and ask why she had turned away and was far.[2]

> "How long, O LORD? Will you forget me forever? How long must I bear pain in my soul, and have sorrow in my heart all day long?" (Ps 13:1–2a).

The Psalms are wonderful companions for a person walking in faith. They allow us to wrestle with God, bring up the big questions and are not shy of accusing God. However, in the end, they always[3] acknowledge that God's plans are not ours, that we can

2. "O God, do not be far from me; o my God, make haste to help me!" (Ps 71:12). This Psalm is similar to Psalm 13. Different is Isa 54. Here Isaiah delivers the word of God saying that God really did turn away from Jerusalem. I wonder how much that is a necessary experience in a time of unimaginable suffering and war. In such times it is, naturally, harder to believe that God is always there. It is easier to explain the darkness on earth as an absence of God: "For a brief moment I abandoned you, but with great compassion I will gather you" (Isa 54:7).

3. There are few exceptions as Psalm 39 ends on a concerning note, as well does Psalm 88.

never know the full story, or the answer to the question why things happen. In the end, the praying person can just look back to the many times when God was close and good and then trust that God will prove to be good again. Also in Psalm 13, the prayer takes a turn in verse 5:

> "But I trusted in your steadfast love; my heart shall re-
> joice in your salvation. I will sing to the LORD, because
> God has dealt bountifully with me" (Ps 13:5–6).

Experiencing a time of God being far, seems to be a normal part of life in faith and trust. We have to trust also in the times when God seems not to be close, trusting that we are always held and embraced by her. In fact, I believe that the moments when we feel God's presence strongly are not the moments when God is very close to us but they are the moments we become aware again of that continual embrace. When you walk with someone holding hands, you do not feel the hand of the other after a while until you start to concentrate on the touch again. I think that is the same with God. The embrace, the hand, they are always there, we are just not always aware of them.

Does God exist? This passage will leave you with the most dissatisfying answer and at the same time with the most wonder-ful: yes, God exists. I cannot prove it, but I just know it. Belief in God is not something you can argue others into. Belief is a gift from God, out of pure and undeserved grace. This gift is sitting there and waiting for many others as well but the way to make them see and embrace this gift is not argument—not to mention force—it is an authentic life that might help them to see. If Chris-tians would concentrate more on living authentic lives that mirror some of the joy we talk about as Christians, instead of trying to be moral detectives who see sin and immorality everywhere, if Christians would be good examples in acknowledging their own sinfulness and dealing with it mercifully in the way they preach that God would deal with it, if Christians would love more than hate, more people would feel drawn to learn more about the source of this happiness and the power that enables them to accept their failures and to strive hopefully towards a higher being.

God is there and his hand is waiting for ours. No one of us would walk this planet, if God had not given his *Yes* for each individual life long before. Often, it is the circumstances, the darkness of human-made hell which some people have to endure and which does not allow them to see the light. And often it is other people, also believers, who get in the way of the Holy Spirit and make it harder for someone to turn to God.

Are not all religions the same? This was the initial question behind which often stand fundamental questions about God. Is there a God? If there is One God, are not all religions the same? Who is that God and why can we not just all pray together . . . ?

This is a very challenging topic. The *modern* heart calls for unity, for the overcoming of boundaries. This is a noble call. In the inter-religious dialogue, it has often been a Christian approach to talk away the differences in the hope to find a compromise. That did more harm to the dialogue than good. Interreligious partners need to know where the other stands. A true dialogue can only happen if the partners make their standpoint clear, accept the differences, and then embrace them. Yes, Jews, Muslims and Christians most probably all pray to the same God. Our ideas about this God and how to live faithfully in the presence of this God have many similarities but also fundamental differences. Which of these are *right* or *wrong*—or maybe all are *right* or all are *wrong*—this will be revealed to us when we stand together before the heavenly throne.

For me as a Christian, I want to be in respectful dialogue with my fellow believers from other religions. I do not want to convince them that my way has to be their way and I would never argue with them that their way was wrong. This does, however, not mean that, in my personal belief system, I am not convinced that Jesus Christ is the way to God but I see my task towards my interreligious siblings not in preaching at them, not in praying for their conversion. I see the task for Christians in praying for them and in praying God's Blessing on them (unconditionally), and in accepting them in love as siblings and children of God. The only acceptable way to *preach* the Gospel to people outside of the Christian belief system for me is simply by trying—which includes failure—by trying to live an authentic Christian life in trust, love, and freedom.

In my belief system, I strongly believe that we are all called to join God's heavenly banquet (more about this also in the chapter about Last Judgment and Hell), but I believe that this way leads through Jesus Christ. I believe in a chance to turn to God once we stand in the presence of God and see clearly, meaning that the earthly death is not the latest possible moment, but that there is a second chance. More about this later.

One of the fundamental differences in the understanding of God is the Christian belief in the Trinity, God three in one, Father, Son, and Holy Spirit / Creator, Redeemer, and Sustainer. This will be the question in the next paragraph.

How can Three be One?

In Basel Cathedral, tour guides would make people get down on their knees; not to worship but to see a very small hidden treasure and beautiful piece of stone masonry. At the foot of a column in the high choir, you can find a little head. It is not a normal head; this one has three noses, three mouths, and four eyes. It is called a *Dreigesicht* (*three-faced head*). One question is: why is this piece of art on floor level. The reason for this is that the floor at the far back of the high choir would not have been there before the big earthquake in Basel in 1356 which destroyed parts of the Cathedral and led to a reconstruction. For us the more interesting question is: what does this piece of art depict?

The Trinity has always been difficult to understand for scholars and for lay people. That Christianity believes in One God, who is Father, Son, and Holy Spirit, all in one but also all separately without being three . . . It must be true. If it was not, who would invent such a complicated idea?

In the first place, this very theoretical belief grew out of a very real experience: people encountered this human being Jesus, a man from Nazareth, and realized that in him they encountered more: the real presence of God, even God herself. How can that be? God was believed to be far from earth, a canyon that could not be bridged in-between God and creation. God must have decided to bridge this gap by becoming human herself. People lived in the expectance of the Messiah, the Anointed, the Christ, who would act in God's power on earth. This Jesus was/is believed to have been this Messiah. If he acted in the power of God, Jesus must have been God's creating word (λόγος—Logos) that has been present before time and gone out from God. Incarnation (the coming into flesh) of this Word, the becoming human of God's Christ was the belief that grew out of this experience. Jesus was the human into whom God had incarnated herself or her creating word that cannot be thought as an own entity (being) but is so strongly connected to God that it is part of God.

The Holy Spirit was seen as the Spirit of God who binds God Father together with God Son, a relational bond of love, and also as the Sprit that binds God and creation together, God and human beings. The Spirit was announced by Jesus when he ascended into heaven as the remaining presence of God on earth once he was united again with the Father in Heaven. Also, the Spirit as person of God was experienced as real and consequently taken into the belief-system. The disciples had come to believe that God was fully present in the person of Jesus. This was the only way they could explain their experiences, their feelings in Jesus's presence. Then, the unexpected happened and Jesus died. There was a feeling of disconnectedness with God; Holy Saturday, Jesus and with him, God, lay in the tomb. On the third day, the disciples experienced the unbelievable: the presence of this Jesus and with him the presence of God had returned. They could feel it, they saw the risen Jesus and could even touch him. God's presence was in their midst again and they experienced this presence so powerfully that there was no doubt that God herself was present. Forty days, so says the tradition, after the first encounter of the disciples with the risen Christ, forty days after Easter, the encounters with the risen Jesus suddenly stopped. The disciples believed that Jesus had ascended into heaven to take his place from where he had come from. The surprise: the disciples could still feel the presence of God fully as when Jesus was in their midst and they remembered the Hebrew Bible talking about the Spirit of God. They remembered Jesus mentioning that the Spirit of God would be with them. That is how the Holy Spirit became one person of the Trinity. God was present with the disciples and God is present with us today, as in the moment when Jesus walked this earth. It is one God who has shown herself to us in different ways.

One God—one head—with three individual but inseparably connected beings in God—three faces. There has also been the attempt to describe the trinitarian God in analogy to water: water is one element but it can be liquid, ice or steam.

The Trinity is not a strange dogma invented by philosophical inspired theology nerds. It is the attempt to make sense of deep spiritual experiences from the early days of humanity's story with this God and, then, especially of experiences of the disciples with God and God's presence in different ways. Many Christians, to this day, experience the presence of the Holy Spirit as life-giving presence. It is not a different God, but it is also not the same like God-Son who walked this earth and it is also not God-Father, it is God-Spirit. In the Eucharistic Prayer, we ask the Holy Spirit to bless the elements of bread and wine, praying that through this Blessing we encounter God-Son in the Body and Blood of Christ. The same God-Son who walked this earth and who sent God Spirit as our advocate and the continuing presence of God on earth.

Does God hear my Prayers?

Prayer is probably the very foundation of a Christian spiritual life. What do you believe happens when you pray? Does God hear your prayers? Does God change because of your prayers? Does God change the course of events? That is, does God intervene in earthly matters, or does prayer just change the person who prays by a change of perspective and by spiritual training? Is God listening at all? And, if God is listening, does God watch from on high and let things go their course? Can we pray for healing? What are our intercessions in church worth anyway? There are many questions about this essential foundation of our very Christian being. There is no answer to these questions. God alone knows. What this chapter can do is to only look at a small number of possible ways to imagine prayer. At the end of the day, what you believe can happen in prayer, comes down to what you believe God can and wants to do in this world. Does God change the course of things or does God stay out? This will be discussed in the next paragraph before we look at different ways to pray.

God's Role in the World

Analyze your prayer. What is the sentence structure? What is it you are asking? Do you tell God things that have happened or are on your heart? Or do you ask God to do something? Ask yourself, what belief of God's role in the world stands behind your way to pray?

In the course of history, there have been uncountable theories about what God's role in the world could be after Creation. Some believe God created the world and withdrew from it, watching from afar and letting things take their course, which he had planted. Others believe God withdrew from actively intervening in the world, but that God is still the sustainer, the giver of life and Spirit. And again others believe that God has never gone far from his creation, staying close, sustaining, taking care and intervening, changing the course of events, healing, rescuing, and giving peace or success.

The latter has increasingly met resistance among theologians. In a world of cliché boxes, this worldview has been pinned to the box with the label *evangelical*. One of the reasons for the resistance, I assume, is that the belief that God intervenes and actively changes the outcome of events, causes the question, *why, then, does God not prevent bad things from happening?* This question, why an almighty God can allow evil in the world and how God can be absolved of this (Theodicy), will be separately discussed later. The challenges this question poses, are probably one reason why many theologians prefer not to believe in a God who intervenes in this world.

Another challenge is the question whether God knows all that will happen and whether he has always known this. If God's mind has always known what will happen, how then could prayer change this eternal mind-set? Or is the evolving creation also an ongoing project for God who does not know where things will go? Has God's decision to create the world and especially humans been a risk taken by God, hoping for the victory of love? Has God's incarnation been a risk: God becoming human, equal among other humans, as a vulnerable child and then a man who met hatred and finally death? Has this always been God's plan? Has it been God's plan all along that Jesus must die? Alternatively, was it an act of love that met hatred, and by God holding on to his love for his people even after the cross, love won and the seed began to grow in the form of many small lights in the world who proclaim and strive to live the Good News of God's love?

Personally, I believe strongly in God's ability and willingness to change things in this world. For me, God is almighty even though God has chosen the power of love over the power of might, violence, the power of armies, and weapons. The power of love sometimes needs longer to win the battle but it eventually wins. I believe that God changes the course of events, protects, prevents, rescues, helps out of dark valleys and sends his angels when necessary. The question whether God changes his mind in these moments or has an unchangeable mind, cannot be answered by any of us and is of minor importance to me. It is one of the mysteries, which might be revealed to us when we are assembled before God's heavenly throne. Absolutely essential, if you hold this belief, is the constant reminder (and this will be repeated in the next section) that prayers are a request not an order. This means, it is in the hands of the One who knows best what should happen. "Grant these prayers, merciful Lord, as is best for us," or as Jesus himself put it: "yet, not my will but yours be done" (Luke 24:42). An *unanswered* prayer is not God letting you down, but so often our wishes are either not for our best or for the best of the bigger plan. Often a closed door or an unanswered prayer will never re-veal their *sense* to us. Sometimes they do, but so often they do not and these are the moments where we need to trust God. *Your will be done.* I do not say this lightly. I know very well that there are situations when our cry for help is about life or death and if this cry remains apparently unanswered it is not easily done with some pious lines about trust and faith. In such existential situations, the Psalms play an important role in my spiritual life. With the Psalms, I do not simply have to accept, I can wrestle with God and cry to God: "Give ear to my words, O LORD; give heed to my sighing. Listen to the sound of my cry, my King and my God, for to you I pray" (Ps 5:1–2).

Prayer

Will you open our meeting in prayer? Will you say grace? Can you pray for me? These are questions that, for some, let the heart jump. "But I don't know how that works," is often the first (understand-able) reply, as if prayer was something that had to follow a certain instruction to be *good* or in order to *work*. This is the speechless-ness St. Paul meant when he wrote, "Likewise the Spirit helps us in our weakness; for we do not know how to pray as we ought" (Rom 8:26a). The speechlessness many of us feel, and most of us have felt before we got more accustomed to praying in a group, is the fear not to say it right, not to say it nicely. Because many public prayers have more become nice poems than real prayers, there is this burden to say *nice* prayers on the spot.

While a prayer, which is beautiful in its language can be won-derful for a meditation, I personally prefer prayers that concen-trate more on the real addressee. For me, perfectly versed prayers sometimes seem more to address those listening with an unspoken attempt to impress than really to bring the deepest desires, hopes and fears of our hearts before God. It reminds me of Jesus's warn-ing not to pray endlessly with empty phrases and especially not to pray just that others see you and are impressed (Mtt 6:5–8).

The Bible does not give an instruction how to pray exactly, does not equip us with a list of requirements for prayer. However, there are some guidelines. We are expected to pray always (1 Thess 5:17; Mark 13:32–37; Mtt 7:7–8 and others). What the content of your prayers might be, we do not learn with the exception of the Lord's Prayer (Mtt 6:9–13; Luke 11:1–13). However, Jesus does not forbid us to bring our hopes and wishes before God (e.g. Mtt 7:7–8). Many theologians discredit this way of prayer. I strongly believe that these deep personal desires (even if they sometimes seem so meaningless), in the context of the whole creation, can also find an ear with God. I think God understands that they are not empty for us. A friend once apologized to me when she told me that she had prayed for good weather for her wedding. Why would you not pray for good weather for your wedding? Do not be mad with God, if it does not happen but in my personal experience, so often God has had a heart for my seemingly small wishes. If I could not share them with God, with whom then? Yes, God "knows what you need before you ask him" (Mtt 6:8b), but your loved one also knows that you love them and you keep telling them, or you wish them a good night every night although they are quite sure that you would want them to have a good sleep without saying it again and again. These things are unnecessary from a theoretical point of view but they are so essential for a relationship and what else is prayer but the way to communicate in our relationship with God?

Many who are new to faith and the whole matter of prayer feel bad and apologetic about the mode of prayer that is an ongoing mumbling with God; little *thank you*, or *please, please, please God* on the way to school, work or while walking the dog, but these are important conversations with God. Not every prayer needs to be nicely structured and in rhyme. A lively and active relationship needs conversation.

Public prayer in a service in church is different from that. The prayers there are said for all present; voiced for them. This needs careful consideration so that as many as possible can find themselves in the prayer and support it with their *Amen*, but public prayers do not need to win a poetry competition in order to be heard by God.

Over time, it makes sense to develop a fixed way of private prayers. The ongoing mumbling is one of my essential ways to communicate with God, but I also discovered the value of fixed set-aside prayer times with words that are given to me: the Psalms. The Daily Offices as this ancient way of prayer is called (i.e. Morning and Evening Prayer) should be as simple as possible but it should comprise (at minimum) a psalm, one reading, a time for intercessory prayer, and the Lord's Prayer. If you do this every day, your relationship with God and your daily life and its structure, will get onto a new level.

The psalms are unique. If you follow a fixed lectionary, it will sometimes happen that a psalm completely matches your feelings: you are grateful and full of joy as you pray Psalm 136 or others. Or you might be sad or angry and pray a psalm that expresses exactly that feeling. However, it will also happen that you pray the opposite of your state of mind. You are happy but the psalm accuses God and wrestles with God or you are sad and the psalm sings praises and rejoices in God's goodness. If that happens, it is so sustaining and healthy for your spirituality and your mental health. It reminds you that times change. It reminds you that every joy also comes to an end and that it should not carry you away too much, but also that every valley of darkness will at one point become brighter again and hope will be restored.

When I lived in a monastery in Jerusalem for nearly a year, the prayer times with the Gregorian Chant of the Psalms were the center of my days. I had mornings when the world seemed to have come to an end and I wanted to scream from pain during the psalms when they were going on and on in praising God but this counter-emotional praying reminded me that I have had uncountable times when I full heartedly joined in these songs of praise and that God was to be praised even in the dark hours of our lives. During times of joyfulness the counter-emotional praying, the wrestling of the psalmist with God, imprinted my deep gratefulness into my soul so that I could remember it in darker moments.

Jesus himself prayed verses of Psalm 22 on the cross (Mtt 27:46b). Strong words: "My God, my God, why have you forsaken me?" It is legitimate to wrestle with God if we feel left alone from God, if the world around us goes to pieces and we see no way out. To wrestle with God means also to stay connected with God. If you argue, if you invest energy into this relationship, it also shows that this relationship means something to you. A faith that allows you to argue with God is mature. God can take it. God prefers an argument over complete silence. A faith that believes you must not give to God anything but praise and thanks is more likely to fall apart in a deep existential crisis. If you believe God is the main power in the world and only worthy to be praised, how do you deal then with the bad things that happen to you? For sure, God is faithful and will reveal herself very often as the one who has been present throughout the crisis, the painful time, but our cry is still legitimate. It is a human experience that God sometimes seems to be far, especially in the times when we need her the most. God is always close, but still we perceive it that way sometimes and this makes it real. Our cry is a plea for God to show herself and let us feel God's presence. For example, after strong accusations and the lamentation of pain and suffering, Psalm 22 eventually expresses trust in God's faithfulness. This is the essence of our hope: not everything bad that happens makes sense, some things will also never make sense from a human perspective, but in all this, we hope and believe that God is not far from us and helps us to get through whatever happens to us. The Psalms provide the tools to reflect on every human situation.

There are so many ways to pray. God loves every prayer, God loves to hear from you, praying for yourself and for others. Praying needs a certain amount of confidence and it will always remain a challenge to pray for the people we do not like or who do not like us—to pray for those who have hurt us or even hate us. But when we pray for them, it will not leave them or us unchanged.

But we also need enough time to pray for ourselves. It is important to find a balance. There are times for everything, to everything there is a season. Depending how we are feeling, we are more ready to think of the needs of others and there are times when our own needs are top of the list and when we fall into a time of speechlessness. This is when we need to remember that God knows our hearts and understands us even without words. In fact, many would claim that silence, being still before God, is the deepest and most intimate of all modes of prayer. Personally, I would not want to make up a "prayer hierarchy," but, for sure, silence is so essential for a healthy spiritual life. It is into the silence that God can speak and not just listen to you and it is in the silence that you can hear. It is a question of your personality. Some people would write a much longer paragraph about silence than about other modes of prayer, I love silence but cannot only have silence or too much of it.

Whichever way you find, remember, God and you are in a relationship and prayer is your way to communicate. It is like in a love relationship or a very good friendship: it often does not matter so much what you do, whether you discuss something, tell the other how beautiful they are, argue, or sit in silence. The main point is to spend time together.

How can there be suffering in the World, if there is a God? (Theodicy)

The theological/philosophical name for this question is Theodicy, which goes via French back to Greek and contains two words: God (θεός—théos) and Justice (δίκη—diké). When we talk about this question, God stands in the dock. Nothing less is in question but God's justice. How can there be suffering in the world, if you are in charge, God?

If God is almighty, then God potentially has the ability to prevent evil from happening. "Does God not want to destroy evil?" "Is God not almighty?" Both would be hard to accept for believers. There is even a third option, probably the hardest from all: "If everything comes from God, does evil also come from God?" That is the explanation some of the authors and prophets of the Bible have chosen in order to make sense of catastrophes, lost wars, the

Babylonian exile, et cetera. In this case God would use evil—would use war and disease—to teach creation or to punish creation for not obeying God's commandments.

All options are not very encouraging. You can start balancing pros and cons. Well, a weak God is not much help to anyone, so maybe it is more comfortable to believe that we are fully at the mercy of the God whom we have experienced as gracious so many times, even if we receive evil from him. Martin Luther took this standpoint. There is more hope in believing that all good and all evil comes from our gracious and almighty God than believing that some evil forces are out of control and do with us what they want.

Still, this is a very painful standpoint to take. It might be true for some people that pain they went through at one point in their lives *makes sense* when looking back much later. I am always skeptical and careful with this idea of *it needed to be, it all made sense.* Bless them, who can accept harm, pain and other difficulties or even horrors in their lives. If you have just lost your child, you do not want anyone to tell you that it will make sense one day and you do not even want to imagine that there could be any sense in this.

Before I start to develop my theological standpoint on this, it is important to make it very clear: no one has ever developed a fully satisfying answer to this question and we will not until we stand before the heavenly throne. The only thing we can do is to look at the different options our human mind can think of. The issue is to bring together our experience of a loving God with powers beyond imagination and our experience of real existing suffering and pain in our lives and the world. We can only look at different options and different theological concepts and there will be different ways of knitting these options together. The following is my personal knitting that at one point will remain unfinished and leave this mystery to God alone.

I believe that God is almighty, nothing on earth nor heaven happens without God knowing it. I believe that God created this world and humans and made the free decision to give them a certain freedom of choice. God loves all of creation and every single human being in particular. Each human is free to return this love or to reject it, even violate it. God would be free to intervene but freely decides to uphold the principle of human freedom to act differently than intended in God's plan.

This would explain how there can be human violence and human-made suffering. There are also natural disasters and diseases of which some have a human authorship (think of Climate Change or all the human-made influences on our bodies) but still many have not. What is the driving force behind them? My concept from above cannot explain this. My concept also cannot withstand human tragedy of incomprehensible scale like the Holocaust or wars. The idea of God holding on to self-made principles while having the ability to do something is horrible. Therefore, yes, I believe in what I wrote above but there needs to be more. The blank, the mysterious part is too painful in that explanation to be left alone like this.

The theologian who has influenced me a lot and helped me to dive deeper into this mystery is Jürgen Moltmann (*1926). His book, *The Crucified God*,[4] does not so much answer the question why evil happens but asks the question: where is God in this? Where is God in the suffering of the world? Right in the midst of it. Does God watch unmoved from heaven above or does God not even notice? No, there is suffering in God when creation suffers and God does not stay far or above suffering but like God himself went to the cross and suffered, so God is present with the suffering and shares in their suffering. For a long time, there has been the strong theological principle that God cannot suffer whatsoever; there even was the theory that in the moment of Jesus's suffering on the cross, God left the human Jesus and watched from the outside (became known as the heretical teaching of *Docetism*). Maybe I would not say that God suffers but that there is suffering in God.[5] Not to draw a picture of God that is too anthropomorphic

4. Moltmann, *Der Gekreuzigte Gott*.

5. This is more an in-depth theological/philosophical question. Suffering can change the very core of ones being, can rule over a human. I would not say that God's very being is changed by suffering or that God loses control like

(humanlike) but I cannot imagine God remaining unmoved with what happens on earth. I believe God is right next to us when we suffer, is right next to the people of Syria when the bombs fall again, is right with the exploited child, the slave sex-workers, the cancer patient, the grieving. God is right there, far away from the heavenly comfort-zone.

This does not explain, why there is suffering in the world, why God does not end it (not yet or not all at once at least), but it helps me to believe that God cares deeply. It also emphasizes the importance of our role as lights in the world. Jesus empowered us to continue the preparation of the coming Kingdom of God. It is our task to make a difference in this world so that the Kingdom of God, which has begun in Jesus Christ, can grow and when Christ comes again, be fully brought about.

---

humans can when suffering. That is why I prefer the idea that there is suffering *in* God.

IV

Are we really all Sinners?

OR: ANTHROPOLOGY

THERE IT IS, THIS strange couple with the telling names *Adam* (earth) and *Eve* (the life-giving). The Bible portrays them living in a lush garden that provides them with everything and, like children from very rich families, who sometimes turn rebellious out of the boredom of having everything, Adam and Eve decide to break the one rule God had given them:

> "You may freely eat of every tree of the garden; but of the tree of the knowledge of good and evil you shall not eat, for in the day that you eat of it you shall die" (Gen 2:16b–17).[1]

God planted all the trees in the garden and two are named explicitly: *the tree of life* and the *tree of the knowledge of good and evil* (Gen 2:9). The day, they would eat from the tree of the knowledge of good and evil, God threatens them with death. The serpent now cleverly convinces Eve that the tree is fully in line with

---

1. "From all the edible trees of the garden eat and from the tree of knowledge (or: insight/understanding) of good and evil, you must not eat; for on the day you eat from it, you will die death" (Gen 2:16b–17, AS).

the food-safe regulations and even desirable because its fruit will make Adam and Eve like God (Gen 3:4–5).

There are a number of things, which need to be noted here:

1. There are two explicitly mentioned trees. The tree they ate from was the *tree of knowledge of good and evil*. The reason why they are thrown out of Paradise is God's fear that they might also want to eat from the *tree of life* (Gen 3:22b).

2. Interestingly, God had never forbidden them to eat from the *tree of life*. It was Eve who told the serpent that God had forbidden to eat from *the tree that is in the middle of the garden* (Gen 3:3). Now, when the two trees are introduced, the Hebrew is not very clear on the point which of them is in the middle of the garden or whether both are in the middle of the garden (Gen 2:9b).[2] However, it is interesting that Eve widened God's prohibition and God comes back to her with a stricter interpretation of his own prohibition.

3. We should note that the text never mentions an apple. That is a later misunderstanding.

Why all this about Adam and Eve and trees and garden? Out of this story, later theologians—very prominent among them Augustine—developed the concept of the *Original Sin*. The idea is that by breaking God's law, Adam and Eve caused an unfixable break in the relationship between humans and God and this curse, this sin of being far from God's will, could be transferred from human being to human being through the sexual act and giving birth. This line of theology has had horrible consequences for millennia and has led to more and more theories and a completely messed up morality. To top it all off, women were blamed for deceiving men and causing all this misery. So the legend has also served the male dominated church as argument for why women could not be entrusted with authority over anything, not even over themselves.

---

2. וְעֵץ הַחַיִּים בְּתוֹךְ הַגָּן וְעֵץ הַדַּעַת טוֹב וָרָע׃ (wə·ʿêṣ ha·ḥay·yîm bə·tō·wk hag·gān wə·ʿêṣ had·da·ʿat ṭō·wḇ wā·rāʿ.)

This story has been abused as an argument for the suppression of women for hundreds of years.

Again, it was Basel Cathedral and her wise stonemasons who helped me to deepen my own theology and understanding of this story at the beginning of our Bible. Just two columns north of the trinity depiction mentioned above, you find four depictions concerning the topic of *Original Sin*. Three are easy to identify. You find a naked man, a naked woman, a tree, a serpent and a piece of fruit, then the same people with fig leaves covering their shame and you see them being thrown out of the garden by an angel with a sword. The fourth depiction has always been a riddle to me. This panel shows two beasts with the bodies of a lion and eagle's heads carrying a man in something that looks like a hammock in between them. I learned that this is supposed to depict the ascension of Alexander the Great.[3] There is a legend about this young successful Macedonian king who had conquered most of the known world, as far as todays Pakistan, at an age when many young people today are thinking of their driver's license. The legend tells us that at the pinnacle of his success, Alexander wanted a number of beasts to take him up to heaven so that he might be numbered among the Gods. Even though he was nearly as powerful as many Ancient people would have imagined a God to be, it did not work and he returned to earth.

What does this legend have to do with Adam and Eve eating their fruit? For me this was eye opening. The so-called *Original Sin* is not about eating that fruit, and not even so much about their disobedience to God. The real sin of all human beings, which is passed on from one generation to the next, is the deep inner wish and attempt to be like God. Humans want to put themselves in the position of God. Humans want to know about good and evil. Most Church Fathers saw this ability as a gift. I doubt it is. Humans do not use it so much to correct their own misdoings but rather to judge that of others. If others do not commit something evil, then we declare them evil by some random criteria like skin color,

3. You find this in other churches as well, for example in the Münster in Freiburg im Breisgau.

gender, nationality, race, sexual orientation, political background, divorced, remarried . . . Only God is allowed to judge about the core of our very being, only God can really judge about Good or Evil. This is not to say, our legal systems in working democracies are all wrong. There is a difference between judging a behavior that threatens the well-being of society (murder, theft; even though the quality and wisdom of the laws influences the quality of jurisdiction) and judging between Good and Evil.

Humans want to judge, humans want to be the ones to label others, and humans try to replace God: they treat the earth like their own possession, even though they are just stewards, they kill others and end lives that God has destined to prosper, they muddle with DNA and think about selecting embryos according to our human liking and wish list.

God was right: humans would have stretched out their arm to eat from the *tree of life* as well. If we could take the pill to live forever, I guess most of us would.

This is, in my belief, *Original Sin*, the sin Adam and Eve committed as first people and all generations shared in this sin by the same behavior. Alexander *the Great* judged over life and death, Good and Evil and ruled over most parts of the known world, so he thought he could move to his appropriate palace in heaven and be God himself.

There is this big philosophical and theological question whether this makes humans evil all over and as a part of their nature. *homo homini lupus est,*[4] wrote the Roman comedian Plautus (third and second century BC) and also the sixteenth and seventeenth-century philosopher Thomas Hobbes. Thomas Hobbes believed that humans (he was mainly talking about politics and states) are evil by nature and if not controlled by hard laws and government, they kill each other all the time.

The church has had a certain empathy for this negative anthropology (science of human behavior). We live in the dilemma that the events in the world sometimes seem to prove this position

---

4. Plautus wrote: *lupus est homo homini.* The Thomas Hobbes word order is just much more popular. It means: A human is a wolf to another human.

right. However, in all the darkness, there are many spots of light; some of them shining so bright that the darkness seems less dark from time to time. In addition, as Christians we believe that God has created all things and if God is the ultimate Goodness, how could something that comes from her be not good? God herself declared in the story of Creation that everything was "very good" (Gen 1:31). Here we are again at the point of the unsolved question how evil came into the world and how it can ravage in this world.

Even if humans are not evil by nature and definitely not totally evil or evil through and through, none of us is perfect. Some of us have done very bad things in our lives and carry a lot of guilt on our shoulders. Definitely all of us have done bad things, hurt people, disappointed them, tricked them or whatever. None of us is without sin and it would be a sin to think you are sinless. ("If we say that we have no sin, we deceive ourselves, and the truth is not in us," 1 John 1:8).

After Jesus was baptized by John the Baptist, he went into the wilderness. The Gospels tell us that he fasted for forty days and by the end was—naturally—very hungry. It was then that Satan came to him and tempted him. First, Satan wanted Jesus to turn stones into bread, saying, "If you are the Son of God, command these stones to become loaves of bread" (Mtt 4:3b). Jesus replied with another Bible verse, then, Satan puts him on the pinnacle of the temple saying, "If you are the Son of God, throw yourself down; for it is written, 'He will command his angels concerning you,' and 'On their hands they will bear you up, so that you will not dash your foot against a stone'" (Mtt 4:6). At last, Satan took Jesus on a high mountain to show him all the kingdoms of the world and said to Jesus, "All these I will give you, if you will fall down and worship me" (Mtt 4:8–9).

This is a real theological argumentation with both sides throwing Bible verses at each other. Apart from that, this passage never gave me much more than admiration of Jesus's perseverance and humbleness until I started to picture what was happening differently.

When you close your eyes and picture this story, what do you see? Do you, also, see Jesus standing in the desert somewhere with a man next to him, with or without horns or so? What changes, if you imagine Jesus alone and the temptation is that voice in his head that we all know; that voice that pops up and brings thoughts we do not like and with which our other inner conscious voice argues?

There he is, Jesus, the human from Nazareth. He had just been baptized and something deeply spiritual has happened there; something that witnesses described as the heavens being open and God's voice calling Jesus "the beloved" (Mtt 3:17b). There he is. He had always had a special relationship to God but this made him wonder who he really was. Maybe he was the Messiah, everyone was waiting for, maybe he was the Son of God? I believe, like many others, that Jesus discovered his vocation and him being the Son of God gradually. Now when he was in the desert after his Baptism, maybe Satan was this voice in his head saying things as, *Maybe you are the Son of God. So, why do you not try and turn these stones into bread?* Or: *if you are the Son of God, you could rule the kingdoms of the world.* Maybe Jesus's temptation was so very human; simply this voice in his head that was not humble at all and dreamed of power and being special. Jesus resisted.

This voice is not necessarily sin; it all depends what you do with this voice. Do you let it prevail or do you argue with it and silence it like Jesus did? This voice is often also the voice that discriminates against others, that brings up racist arguments, homophobic ideas, that belittles women. The Diocese of New Westminster stopped calling their Racism Awareness seminars *Anti-Racism Training.* They are now called *Dismantling Racism* and rightly so. No seminar can silence this inner voice that comes up with racist ideas. I would go so far as to say that everyone has this voice about people with other ethnic backgrounds or people who live their *different* sexual orientation openly.[5] What do you do with it? Are you aware of this voice and its evil and do you let it be or do you reject it? This is the narrow ridge between sin and not

5. A recommendation for further reading is: Diangelo, *White Fragility.*

sinning. This voice needs to be dismantled. We need to be aware of it and learn to control it so that we do not act on its assumptions and we need a place where we can lay down our feeling of guilt for having such a voice or for the situations where we gave in to it and let the voice turn into action or a real spoken harmful word.

Many churches have it as their regular custom to confess their sins, either individually or all together in a service in church. Many *modern* people do not like this part because it is so countercultural. Individuality is the *non-plus-ultra* at the moment. You can do everything and everything is about you. To acknowledge that this individual, that I am a sinner and actually not worthy to stand in God's presence if he had not made me worthy, can be painful, but it can also be so freeing. No, we are not perfect and we do not have to be perfect. God knows us and the only thing God wants from us is that we are aware of ourselves and try to do better. But if we fail, God forgives. How many times do you give in to this inner voice? Why is this inner voice there anyway? Bring it and lift it up to God and God promises to help you to grow. We are accepted as we are, thanks to God's act of Love. We are *saved* would be the traditional way to put it. What that might mean will be explored in the next chapter.

V

Do you believe that Jesus existed?

OR: CHRISTOLOGY AND SOTERIOLOGY

Do you believe that Jesus existed?

IF IT IS NOT the question: *Do you believe in the Bible?*, then, *Do you believe that Jesus existed?* is often this question that will likely come up in a conversation with someone who has just learned that you are a believing Christian. For many people, the point of believing in Jesus is the equivalent of believing in the existence of Jesus. However, the question of Jesus's existence is not a question of belief. The existence of Jesus is a precondition for Christian belief but it is not a question of belief or faith. The human person, Jesus of Nazareth, is so very well documented—more than most of his contemporaries and other people in antiquity. The existence of most contemporaries is seen as probable if we have one source that mentions them. If it is two sources, the better. It is enough that their name is mentioned and maybe the place where they are from. With regard to Jesus we have extensive literature that was—for the standards of antiquity—written relatively close to his life. We do not only have the many individual writings that were collected in the New Testament, but there are also non-canonical writings and even writings from non-Christian writers: e.g. Josephus and as early as app. fifty AD there was an incident in Rome with Christians involved, about which we learn from the Roman first century historian Suetonius.[1]

The big difference between Jesus and his historical contemporaries (regarded by some as having similar importance) is that many (but not all) of them left their own writings (think of Julius Caesar, Octavian, Josephus, Philo). Despite this, Jesus and his historical existence is extremely well documented and most secular historians do not question it.

The question with Jesus is not about believing whether he existed. The question with Jesus is who he was. Was Jesus the son of Mary and a carpenter (or builder) from Nazareth and a preacher, period, *or* was Jesus a man from Nazareth, the son of Mary, who grew up as son of a carpenter (or builder) from Nazareth and was God present in him in a way beyond anything the world has ever experienced before? That is the question of belief, of faith. The mere historical existence of the person Jesus is not a matter of question.

Why did Jesus say so many nasty things?

This question does not come up often but depending on the lectionary a church uses, sometimes —often in summer—there is one Sunday after the other when the appointed Gospel is one of the more challenging passages of Jesus. The ways to deal with these often disturbing and harsh quotes are manifold. For example, some churches decide to take them out of their lectionary or, some priests might have them read and then preach on the Hebrew Bible reading for the day. If people preach about these texts, some take them literally, some take them as analogies, some say Jesus never said this, some say Jesus meant it all differently and there are so many more ways to deal with them.

1. Suetonius, *The Live of Claudius*, 25:4: "Since the Jews constantly made disturbances at the instigation of Chrestus, he expelled them from Rome."

"If someone comes to me and does not hate/is indifferent to their father, mother, daughter, their wife, children, brothers, sisters, and also life itself, they cannot be my disciples" (Luke 14:26, AS).

"Do not assume that I have come to throw/to sow peace unto/on earth; I have not come to throw peace but a sword" (Mtt 10:34, AS).

What do we do with these? Jesus said many more things that are challenging. Jesus spoke about leaving everything behind including possessions or even the burial of one's own father, Jesus spoke about it being better to lose an arm or an eye than . . . , he treats a Syro-Phoenician woman very badly (racist even I would say). Somehow, such harsh words do not go well with *my Jesus.* Each of these passages needs an individual interpretation and it is hard to cover them all together as *all the difficult quotes from Jesus.*

What the existence of these does tell us and also the fact that we are so unsettled and every time anew surprised that they exist, is that our internal image of Jesus might have moved quite far from who Jesus really was. As mentioned before, each of these passages needs an interpretation of its own but the blond, super kind and child-hugging Jesus who blushes when someone says something naughty in his presence and who speaks with an angel's voice words of poetry always about love, this Jesus is not the Jesus we find in the Bible and it is most definitely not very close to the real Jesus.

Jesus was unsettling. Jesus was revolutionary, provoking, shocking people with his message. *The Kingdom of God is at hand* sounds so nice to people who have heard this sentence over and over again. We have domesticated Jesus and his message. It was not just nice for the people who heard him preach. They were deeply shaken, awe-struck by the possibility of God's Kingdom being at hand. Jesus's social teachings, as well, undermined the teaching of the religious elite and spoke clearly to the people who heard him.

I strongly believe that these tough quotes that have been kept for us in the Gospels, are fully authentic; maybe they are even the most authentic ones. They would at all times have unsettled people and been hard to explain. Why should the authors of the Gospels who had a genuine interest in *selling* the Jesus story well, why should they have added—in the sense of invented—these completely counterproductive statements? Their job would have been easier without them but maybe they felt that they could not leave them out without moving too far from the real Jesus. This Jesus knew how to shake people and if we want to be relevant in today's society with our Christian message, we have to learn again to be shaken ourselves, to be unsettled by what we hear and read. The Gospel is not simply a nice and easy story about a nice man, it is a world-changing report by people who have experienced the real presence of almighty God in action in this world preaching to them that God is faithful despite the sins of the world.

> "Whoever comes to me and does not hate father and mother, wife and children, brothers and sisters, yes, and even life itself, cannot be my disciple . . . So therefore, none of you can become my disciple if you do not give up all your possessions" (Luke 14:25–33).

Whoever could sign such a statement right away must have a very painful relationship with their parents, partner or their own children. Jesus would have either very few disciples or a very grim and emotionally hurt bunch of people. What did he mean? Most would agree, that Jesus wants to make one thing very clear here: the Kingdom of God has ultimate priority. There are three ways forward from there:

1. You are satisfied with this metaphorical core meaning of his words and carry on;

2. You look at the Greek and find that μισέω (miseo) can also be translated with *being indifferent* instead of *to hate*;

3. You stay with the text for a while and wrestle with it.

Why could it be of interest for Jesus that his followers hate their families or are indifferent to them? What did it mean to become a disciple? It meant that you had to leave your home to follow a preacher who could not even guarantee your daily bread. It meant that you had to join a preacher who was in constant conflict with the powerful authorities: spiritual and political authorities. It also meant that your family faced social marginalization, as they were held responsible for your lack of judgment. As family, there were all kinds of good reasons to stop you from following this outlaw. Jesus knew this; even from his own family. He brings this up right away to all who consider following him. You must know that your family will try to stop you and that you will have to choose between them and me.

The world has changed for many of us. When you decide to go to church on Sundays and live a Christian life, many parents, partners or children will not intervene, and might even support you. Is there a need to *hate* them in order to be a good Christian? No, of course not. Jesus would attack the Pharisees for having ways to get around the commandment to honor father and mother:

> "And why do you break the commandment of God for the sake of your tradition? For God said, 'Honor your father and your mother,' and, 'Whoever speaks evil of father or mother must surely die.' But you say . . . So, for the sake of your tradition, you make void the word of God. You hypocrites!" (Mtt 15:3b–7a).

For Jesus, the *commandment of God* is to honor father and mother. His words about the necessity to hate one's family is built into a condition: the first commandment is to love "God with all your heart, and with all your soul, and with all your might" (Deut 6:5). This is the absolute commandment without *but*. Now, if your family tries to prevent you from following God, from becoming a disciple of Jesus, then, but only then, Jesus demands a choice: you want to follow God, your family does not let you, then decide. Jesus does not allow for a fifty-fifty discipleship. In this way, I would also read his tough call to let the "dead burry their own dead" (Mtt 8:22b).

This is a tough call and a true and honest exegesis (critical interpretation) of the Gospel should not try to smoothen it. To follow Jesus is a radical vocation. For many people, the world has changed and resistance in families is small. However, for other people in the world, things have not changed and becoming Christian is still equal to dying to their social surroundings—or even literally. Following Christ, with heart and soul, has mostly and throughout the times of this creation been counter to the social mainstream. Even in the times which are now often praised as the golden times of the church, such as the Middle Ages, it was against the mainstream to stand up for the poor, to treat every human being as equal before God, and to make love and compassion the major guidelines in one's life.

> "Do not think that I have come to bring peace to the earth; I have not come to bring peace, but a sword" (Mtt 10:34).

This is probably the most popular verse when someone wants to undermine the goodness of Jesus. It is indeed something not to read over quickly. It is another statement from Jesus, which I would consider as highly authentic. It would not do this expression any justice by finding an easy way out. At the same time, as with the verse discussed above, it should not be read as a commandment. It is not Jesus's aim to turn family members into enemies but it is often the reality. Jesus's coming into the world is like a sword. It is like an early Judgment Day: his coming makes it clear who is for him and who is against him. If family members take different stands on this, the matter has the potential to cut their relationship. It is, yet, another occasion in which Jesus emphasizes the seriousness of his mission and of discipleship. He wants us to be prepared for the possible consequences. It is an act of mercy, a warning, the loud and clear spelling out of the small print. It is, however, not his aim to destroy families.

If it is so hard and dangerous, why should anyone follow Jesus then? The next paragraph will look at this question.

What is the Good News about Jesus?

The church has this annoying habit of using big, often nice-sounding words that serve as answers to every question. How can God be Father, Son, and Holy Spirit and still be one God? Well, that's the *Trinity*. Why did Jesus die on the cross? For our *Salvation*, of course. What is the church's main duty? To proclaim the *Gospel*, the Good News. Everyone in the church, clergy but also parishioners, are good in playing these big cards. Whenever someone offers you such a big word, or concept rather than an explanation for a concrete question, or, you hear yourself using such a word as explanation for something, be brave and ask the question: what does this mean? This will help us all to grow in our understanding of what we actually believe. To be fair to the church and all speaking for her, every profession has its own vocabulary and uses it extensively and naturally. In addition, the church deals with many questions which no one on this side of the heavenly gate can answer clearly. We need language that leaves space for the *holy mystery* and does not nail everything down in detail. The Trinity will always remain a mystery and we can only try to approach it by the use of big concepts or analogies.

What about the Good News? What is it we are proclaiming and what is the Good News about Jesus? Even though I am always careful when everything about faith and God is reduced to the formula (another unclear concept, by the way), *Love*, I still think that the shortest answer to the question about the Good News is Love. God loves his creation and expects creation to respond to this love like a child would respond to the love of their parents: with trust and love in return.

The longer answer consists of several movements:

> Creation—Sustaining the Israelites—Becoming human—Being human—Dying as a human by the hands of humans—Rising from the dead—Ascending into heaven—Sending the Holy Spirit

Often Christians identify the Good News with the New Testament, like in an equation. It is right that the New Testament informs us about essential events in the history of humans and their relationship with God but neither is the New Testament as a whole equal to the Good News, nor is the New Testament alone equal to the Good News.

The Good News start with the beginning of humanity. Without God's will and act of creation this planet would not have become a hospitable place for the development of life, for the gradual development of humans.

> "For it was you who formed my inward parts;
> you knit me together in my mother's womb.
> I praise you, for I am fearfully and wonderfully made"
> (Ps 139:13–14a).

Every single human being can pray these verses. I repeat this: every single human being can pray this. Everyone has been called into life by God. There are no exceptions. No matter where life leads someone, no matter the number of right or wrong choices made in a life, no matter the *luck*, the health, the *success* in a life, each life has received a big *Yes* from God.

God loves his creation. From the first moment, God provided and wished for the well-being of humans, animals, and environment. From the first moment, God's desire was to be in relationship with humans. It was painful for God when humans turned away from him and *left Paradise*. God has always yearned for the restoration of the original relationship and has sent prophets and messengers, holy people to lead God's people.

The Five Books of Moses have one golden thread: the disobedience of God's people, Israel, and God's continuing love and faithfulness. No matter the mercies God showed to the Israelites in Egypt, in the wilderness, in the Promised Land, the Israelites disobeyed God again and again. God reacted with anger from time to time but always turned her face back to them and assured Israel of her faithfulness and love.

When God considered the time right to send the strongest message of her continuing favor and reassurance, God decided to become human herself, become an equal of her beloved children. God made this decision in complete freedom of choice. It was God's free decision to give up divine majesty and invulnerability.

By becoming human, it was also God's free decision to become part of human storytelling, of human memory, and of the misunderstanding and misinterpretation of spoken words.

God became human in the person of Jesus of Nazareth and God became part of this world as it was and is. God did not choose this world because it was perfect and God did not choose a palace and luxury worthy of a divine king as a scene for this Incarnation (literally: coming into flesh). God came into this imperfect world with all its pains, struggles, and injustice. God came to be a healer, to restore the broken relationship between creation and creator, and to bless us humans by his presence among us in human form. Jesus preached this love and called people back into the relationship with God. In him, God gave an example of his love. God's love is sacrificial. God was ready to sacrifice divine power and might to become an equal to us. God sacrificed divine invulnerability and walked the path of a human life with joys, pains, hopes, and anxieties. God did not shy away when his beloved human creation decided to kill him.

It was not, as so often said in old theology, God the Father sacrificing his own son to satisfy himself or some kind of perverse lust for blood. It was God *the Son* giving himself as a sacrifice. The cross was not a necessity planned from God before the beginning of the world. Rather, it was the ugliest accident in creation's history. Humankind turned against their loving God in an act of total sinfulness and judged the highest judge and eventually killed the one and only Lord over life. The circle from Adam and Eve in Paradise who ate from the fruit of the *tree of knowledge of good and evil*, wishing to receive the divine power of judgment, was closed in this enactment of human judgement.

God receives this judgment and suffers death on the cross. This would have been the final seal on humankind's doom but God decided differently. In an act of mercy that passes all understanding, God raised Jesus from the dead not to proclaim the wrath of God but to bring humankind the message of God's continuing faithfulness and the decision to, now, also grant the fruit of the *tree of life*. God decided to give humankind freely from the *tree of life* and to grant humans eternal life in her presence. This closes the circle from creation to the beginning of a new creation. God herself bridged the gap that had grown out of the human turning away from God. The risen Christ promised that he would return to finish what he had begun and to restore God's Kingdom on earth. He left the preparation of this final restoration in the hands of his followers and there it still lies. As Christians we live from the knowledge that God's faithfulness endures forever and that God forgives when we go astray and fall. We live from the hope that our humble steps on this earth will prepare the ground for God's Kingdom of peace on earth little by little until Christ will come again and fulfil the promise when "God will wipe every tear from their eyes [and] death will be no more: mourning and crying and pain will be no more" (Rev 21:4).

As final proof of God's consent to Jesus's proclamation, God let him ascend into heaven before the eyes of the disciples and sent the Holy Spirit as a remaining presence among us; a Holy presence not less real than the presence of God as Jesus of Nazareth. Where the Holy Spirit is at work, God is fully present, touching us, setting hearts on fire, spreading love, healing, and letting life grow and light shine in the darkness.

This, I believe, is the Good News we are called to proclaim and by striving to live accordingly to prepare the ground for God's Kingdom on earth.

VI

Is God really Bread and does Water make us Holy?

Or: The Sacraments

THE EARLY CHRISTIANS OFTEN suffered drastically because of the bloody imagery of one of their rituals. Denunciators would claim that they had seen or heard of a group of Christians performing human (often child-)sacrifices and cannibalism.[1] Is God really bread and wine or are we Christians really cannibals, eating our God?

The church has recognized changing numbers of Sacraments and has also changed its understanding about what a Sacrament is. The churches today still vary in their sacramental theology, in fact, the diverse understanding of the Eucharist is one of the main rocks blocking the stony path to more ecumenical ties between a number of Protestant churches and the Roman Catholic Church. In this chapter, I will follow the Protestant understanding of the number of Sacraments.

---

1. It is one of the sad moments in history where the bullied turned into bullies: Roughly 500 years later, Christians would accuse their Jewish neighbors of exactly the same crime and cause persecution and mass murder on false accusations.

> A Sacrament is "an outward and visible sign of an inward
> and spiritual grace, given to us by Christ himself, as a
> means whereby we receive this grace, and a pledge to as-
> sure us thereof."[2]

A divine promise of grace comes together with a visible and tangible sign (bread, wine, water). However, the church cannot just invent more and more Sacraments, linked to every promise of grace they find in the Bible; it needs to be instituted by Christ—*ordained by Christ himself.*

This is the reason why the churches of the Reformation acknowledge only two Sacraments (Holy Eucharist and Holy Baptism with some debate about Confession as possible third Sacrament). The old tradition knew more Sacraments which all make sense and are to be kept holy, but they were not "ordained by Christ" with any word like: "Do this in remembrance of me" (part of the words of Institution, Luke 22:19b; 1 Cor 11:24b). The Anglican Church decided to follow the argument of the Reformation and acknowledges two Sacraments. However, in order to give reference to the old tradition of seven Sacraments, there is the distinction between *Sacraments* with a capital S and *sacraments* with a lower case s.

Holy Eucharist

The Eucharist / the Last Supper / Holy Communion is the spiritual center for many churches, also in the Anglican Communion. The Anglican Church has seen very diverse and often divisive approaches to the Eucharist over time with times of deep Eucharistic devotion and times when the main service on a Sunday was Matins/Morning Prayer and Holy Communion was only celebrated on rare occasions and special feast days. The status quo is definitely diverse, looking at the worldwide communion; however, the Eucharist has made its way back as the center of Sunday worship in many corners of the Anglican Communion.

---

2. Anglican Church, *Book of Common Prayer,* 550.

What is it we celebrate? What do bread and wine have to do with the Body and Blood of Christ? It all started with Jesus's last supper with his disciples. They came together on the night before he was arrested and had supper together. It depends on the Gospel, whether this was the night before the feast of Passover (the Gospel according to John seems to point to that idea), or whether the Last Supper was, actually, the disciples's Passover meal.

Either way, the symbolism of the Jewish feast of Passover is the context. For Passover, lambs are slaughtered with reference to the time when the Israelites were slaves in Egypt and on the night before they were led into freedom, they were commanded by God through Moses, to slaughter a lamb and mark their doorposts with the blood. This was the sign for the Angel of the Lord to pass by and leave this house with the mark untouched, while the Egyptian households were struck by the death of their first-born children. The lamb loses its life, so that the Israelites may win life and freedom.

At the Last Supper, Jesus took bread and, according to Jewish custom, broke it, prayed over it (*gave thanks*) and then gave it to his disciples. This alone would not have been special or distinct to any other meal they had had before. It was,

1. the fact that this supper happened before the self-sacrifice of Jesus (of God-Son) so that humanity might win life and freedom and lose their fear and slavery of death, finally recognizing the infinite love of God, who is even ready to sacrifice himself. And,

2. Jesus added a word to his distribution of the bread. *This is my body. Do this in remembrance of me.* What exactly he meant by *This is my body,* is the core of many an argument, but in anyway, it adds another dimension to this event of sharing the bread. In addition,

3. he gave the command to repeat this action in remembrance of him. It was the birth of a ritual, remembering Jesus's self-sacrifice on the cross and his presence among the disciples and among the believers in the years to come.

Hoc est enim corpus meum—This is my body. When Christians celebrate the Eucharist or the Last Supper, there are various beliefs what it is that actually happens: is it a ritual of remembrance where the community and the thinking of Jesus strengthen us and help us to go our paths? Is it the sharing of bread and wine in community in which Jesus is really and fully present among the elements of bread and wine and in the community (*Consubstantiation*)? Or do bread and wine change their invisible core, their true being which eyes cannot see, and become body and blood of Christ in the sense of Christ's real presence bound to the elements (*Transubstantiation*)?[3]

The simple answer to this is: no one has the answer to this. It is a question of belief. The Anglican tradition has gone through a number of backs and forths, but has always had the strong line of argument that the question *what* really happens to the elements, cannot be answered by humans. The interest has been more in the question what happens to the believer, when they participate in this celebration and receive the body and blood of Christ.

As core belief, Anglican and Lutheran Churches have always emphasized Christ's real presence in this celebration. Whether Christ is really present in the elements, among the elements or among the people assembled and sharing the elements, has been secondary.

It was the worldwide Corona/Covid-19 pandemic, which brought such questions back to more attention. Can we celebrate online-Eucharistic Services and do believers in front of their TVs and laptops really participate in the mystical presence of Christ or do we need to be present in person and receive the elements?

---

3. Even the belief that the elements change in a mystical way (*Transubstantiation*), does not infer belief that bread and wine turn into real flesh in the carnal sense and the wine into real blood. Because of the deep philosophical and mystical nature of this belief, this misconception has often been the belief the faithful took away. Every scientific examination would still find bread and wine even after the consecration. Maybe it helps to think of a person: there is what your eyes can see, the outside appearance of a person, but what really makes the person is something hidden to the eye and beyond any scientific examination; the real core. The same with the Body and Blood of Christ: they remain bread and wine, but their invisible core of their existence is changed.

Initially, I was against the live-streaming of Eucharistic services. I hold the strong belief that the church should never stop celebrating the Eucharist, even in times of a pandemic when a congregation cannot be present and it had to happen behind closed doors.[4] But I have my questions about how a dispersed community of the faithful can fully participate in the mystical experience of Christ's presence which is so much bound to the reception of the actual elements—the tasting, the sensing, and the in-person experience of community.

I am now more open to the live-streaming, since it lets people participate in the thanksgiving and the praise, even though they are not present in person. I still believe that the actual receiving of at least one of the elements is a vital and essential part of a full participation in Holy Communion, but what this crisis has brought to light again is the fact that—no matter which belief you hold concerning the consecration of bread and wine—the Body of Christ is always more than the elements. The Body of Christ is the church with all its believers. In every celebration of the Eucharist, this Body of Christ is united and stands before God in unity: all the living believers and all who have gone before us and are now with God, they all come together to give praise and thanksgiving in the Eucharist and they are all united with each other and with Christ. Why should this not happen through technological means?[5]

We need to be careful with the theology we promote with that, though. There was a long period in church history, when the number of people who received communion in form of the elements declined constantly until the priest was the only one receiving and

4. It is Anglican dogma that the Eucharistic celebration needs minimum a second person in the congregation, saying the great Amen together with the priest. Personally, I believe that the Holy Spirit does not count people and would bless us, in her infinite grace, with her presence even when the priest offers this celebration on behalf of the church on their own. But again, this is not Anglican consensus.

5. Having written this: I absolutely oppose pre-recorded Eucharistic services. If there is a way to argue about the unification of the faithful across space, the idea that we join a Eucharist that has happened in the past, stretches it too far (even though the Eucharist does go beyond time and unites us with the faithful departed), the core of the ritual is its actuality.

the others just witnessing. This was due to an increasing emphasis on the necessity of purity in the moment of communion. The church wanted to avoid people receiving communion without proper preparation. Over the decades, the result was that people did not dare to receive at all, in order not to be punished for receiving unworthily. During Mass, people would pray the Rosary while the priest was saying the prayers at the altar silently. Only when the bells rang and the priest elevated the consecrated host, would the people look up, kneeling and feasting on the sight of the Lord present in the elements, but they would not receive. The church should by all means avoid going into a direction that enacts the Eucharist as a show happening on its own between priest and God, while the others only act as witnesses. Live-streamed Eucharistic services could send such a message.[6]

Now, what is the Eucharist? The name tells part of it: it is giving thanks. The people bring their sacrifices of thanks and praise and God, in his Grace, gives the gift of Christ's full presence by the power of the Holy Spirit.

communion, encounter, taking-in

We stand in communion before God, we lay down all we have in our personal backpacks, trusting that God knows what we bring and what weighs heavy on our shoulders, and we open us up for an encounter with God. In the Eucharist, the living Christ meets us, greets us and blesses us. If you are open for the mystical experience, you can feel the embrace of God in this celebration, the gentle touch of Christ who blesses you. The receiving of the elements, the sensual taking-in of Christ's presence is your *yes* to God's presence in your life and in you. Every time, you come to the altar to receive God, God takes more room in you, and like the bread and wine become part of you, God becomes part of you and you, step by step, more like God.

6. I am also not a supporter of the idea to invite people to have bread and wine on their living-room table while watching the Eucharist online and then to consume the (I think) non-consecrated elements. But at the same time: who am I to say what the Holy Spirit can or cannot do?!

It is food. This means, to receive it once is not enough. We need regular meals for the way. As believers, we need the reassurance of God's presence and God's promises. The Eucharist has this interesting duality: it is all about you and God, your relationship, trust, love, interaction. At the same time, it is all about the community. In the Eucharistic celebration, the whole broken Body of Christ is assembled and united, and the bond between us and our siblings in faith renewed.

Flesh and Blood? Really? Yes, to be fair, the symbolism of flesh and blood is not always helpful. It is easy to imagine some kind of cannibalism—Christians eating their God. However, the image of the Body of Christ for the entirety of the church with all its faithful is beautiful. Each and every one of us has a part to play in this body, else the rest does not function. Also, the mystical experience of receiving Christ, literally, into our very being, by receiving his body and blood, is so powerful, that I would never want to give up on it.

For the Ecumenical discourse, my hope is that at least all churches, which profess the real presence of Christ in the Eucharist, will come to a consensus that this is the core and minimal consensus for shared celebrations. It is about the receiving of Christ in community with the Saints and faithful, undeserved and out of grace alone.

The *Leuenberg Concord*, a document that sealed the full communion between the European Lutheran and Reformed Churches[7] in the 1970s, signed at Leuenberg, Switzerland, close to Basel, agreed that the means in which Christ is present in the elements is secondary. Important is that we believe in Christ's presence.

And I believe that the Holy Spirit, who blesses the elements for us solely out of grace, will also be generous enough to grant the individual believer the kind of presence, they pray for: if you are from the Reformed tradition and believe in Christ's presence among the people gathered, I am sure you will find Christ in your midst. If you believe in Christ's presence among the elements, you will find him. If you believe that the elements change their core

---

7. Not the Anglican Churches.

being and become Christ's spiritual body, you will find Christ in every crumb of the consecrated host and in every drop from the chalice.

The Eucharist is God's gift for us. It is a celebration: life wins over death, love over hate and God meets us where we are and where we need God. St. Thomas needed to touch the wounds of Jesus with his fingers in order to believe. God granted him this experience; God met him where he was and met him in the way he needed in order to believe. I believe that also for the way in which God meets us in the elements and the celebration. God meets us in the way we need. I also believe, that some of us need the mystical touch of God in the celebration of Holy Eucharist while others can fully prosper in the word alone. For many it needs the fullness of God's grace of the Christian spiritual tradition and rituals with all their symbolism, others can spiritually prosper without the full spectrum of symbolism. Both are fine; neither is superior.

Holy Baptism

Does water make us holy? Baptism is an interesting Sacrament. In the Middle Ages and the Early Modern times, parents would send the God-mother or the God-father with the new-born baby wrapped in blankets and often just a day old to church to have the child baptized. There was a high child mortality and parents were afraid that the child would be rejected entry into heaven, if it died without having received the Sacrament. Martin Luther and Hyldrich Zwingli were arguing in the sixteenth century whether something really happens in the moment of Baptism. While Luther saw it as a sacramental act where outward sign and inward invisible grace came together, Zwingli argued that Baptism was just the outward sign for something that had already happened.

But what is it that happens in Baptism? Let us start with the simple fact: Baptism is the initiation rite of Christianity. This means that Baptism is the moment when a person becomes a Christian. Thanks to St. Augustine, we still carry the idea that the child needs Baptism so that our *Original Sin*, the sin we are supposed to have inherited from Adam and Eve, is washed away. St. Paul prepared the ground for this when he wrote,

> "Do you not know that all of us who have been baptized into Christ Jesus were baptized into his death? Therefore, we have been buried with him by baptism into death, so that, just as Christ was raised from the dead by the glory of the Father, so we too might walk in newness of life" (Rom 6:3–4).

Baptism is believed to be a new beginning, even if the candidate is a baby. You enter a new realm, you swear allegiance to another King, namely Christ. By becoming part of his realm, you are taken into the life-giving power of Divine Love, which was set free by the self-sacrifice of God on the cross. You join the covenant between God and her beloved people and receive the Holy Spirit into your life—the Holy Spirit who helps you to strive for a life where sin and evil desires do not get the last word, but where reconciliation, forgiveness and a continuing transformation of the heart of the believer are the ruling principles.

Now, what happens in Baptism? The water is a symbol of purification. We take off our clothes (that was the old tradition), the old burden, and in the act of the pouring over of water or the immersion into the water, receive the Holy Spirit in our hearts.

I love to think about Baptism in yet another way. In earlier times, the church often had the baptismal font at the Western portal of the church. Many of the old churches were built as depictions of the human life. You enter through the portal in the West, symbolizing birth. Then, you pass the baptismal font, the entry of the person into the covenant with God. From that moment, you walk hand in hand with God, step by step, along the nave facing East. These churches had the concept that the further East you got, the holier the space. At one point, there would have been a screen preventing you from entering the holiest space in the church, the High Choir with the High Altar. There, the clergy would celebrate the Eucharist facing East towards the rising sun. The rising sun has been a symbol for Christ, the light of the world, since antiquity.

Every day, the sun comes again faithfully in the East, like Christians are awaiting the coming of Christ again.

Now, it is possible that you might pass the baptismal font and walk this path on your own. I believe the hand of God would still be there to guide you. I also believe that every human being has been called into life by God long before their birth and been taken into the covenant of love with God. I do not believe that the old language and idea that Baptism is about salvation and being *in* or *out* are helpful anymore. What is the difference then? Why should we continue to baptize people?

Holy Baptism remains absolutely central for me. For me, it is the moment when a person or the representatives (often parents and godparents) ley their hands into the already outstretched hand of God and say, *yes, guide me.* For me, Baptism makes all the difference. Imagine a mother and her child. The mother loves the child more than anything from the very first moment to the last, no matter what. Child and mother walk along and the mother loves the child unconditionally. Baptism is for God the moment when the child looks into their mother's eyes and says: "I love you too!" The mother would love the child even if the child never said this in all their life, but how much stronger is the bond of love after this magic, mystical moment! "I love you too!" God calls us into being, God cares for us with a love beyond our understanding and God loves every human being, no matter what. Baptism is the moment, when this love is returned; when the human says: "God, I love you too!"

Does water make us holy? No, it does not. It is the bond of love that becomes a full circle in this beautiful rite of Baptism and that gives us a holiness which you can sense like you can sense a strong bond of love between a parent and their child.

VII

What happens after the End of my Retirement?

OR: ESCHATOLOGY

NOW WE GET TO the delight of every preacher: Fire and Brimstone, Judgement, Hell and Damnation. What better topic could you think of to prepare the listening congregation for the *Happy Sunday*-greeting at the church door after the service? The topics Last Judgement, Heaven and Hell (for hell often: Gehenna or Hades) and the Second Coming of the Christ are very common in the Bible. The simple statement: *I do not believe in hell*, does not usually satisfy me. If we do not believe in hell (of course, we all now have the horned devil in a smoky chamber in mind with a lot of torture instruments and fire around him), well, if we do not believe in hell, what do we do with the biblical passages which speak about it? The same with the Last Judgment which is very present in Jesus's parables and talks, especially so in Matthew.

Last Judgement

> "Then I saw a great white throne and the one who sat on it; the earth and the heaven fled from his presence, and

no place was found for them. And I saw the dead, great and small, standing before the throne, and books were opened. Also another book was opened, the book of life. And the dead were judged according to their works, as recorded in the books" (Rev 20:11–12).

"When the Son of Man comes in his glory, and all the angels with him, then he will sit on the throne of his glory. All the nations will be gathered before him, and he will separate people one from another as a shepherd separates the sheep from the goats, and he will put the sheep at his right hand and the goats at the left" (Mtt 25:31–33).

The fear to fail in the moment of this judgement has had its impact on the lives of so many of our ancestors and still has on many Christians today. Why are we afraid of the idea of judgement, of giving account of our doings in life? I guess that even though it has become unpopular to think of ourselves as sinners who are not always perfect and who do not always act to the best of everyone, who are driven by thoughts and motivations which we do not like ourselves, we are quite aware that no one would only have positive entries in this so-called *Book of Life*. It is this idea that in the moment of judgement, the case is closed, the book finished and it seems like there was no way to improve our situation once we have been ordered into this heavenly courtroom. Even if we somehow came to believe that we would do quite well in this courtroom, we look at our neighbors, our friends and think: O, I do not want them to do badly and be rejected entry to Heaven.

It is, actually, quite a privilege to think like this. I would say that it is much easier to think so generously about the salvation of all in a Western and white culture, where most people do not have real enemies, no one to be afraid of, are not suffering from the loss of close relatives and friends due to war (not disregarding the many people who do suffer under the hands of others or the system in Western culture). If you live in Syria, Palestine, in a civil war country or if you live in a western country but are discriminated against every day because of your skin color or are treated as nonexistent because your bed is the pavement, it is a much bigger step to wish for the salvation of all than to see the prospect of a moment when justice is executed as a source of hope. It is inconvenient but it needs to be respected that in every situation where injustice seems to win over justice, the hope of the Last Judgement as the one moment when things are set right, is completely human and naturally a source of strength to go on. It might even be a source that enables forgiveness in the knowledge that the restoration of justice is with God and in good hands.

Still, I hold another belief. I believe in Last Judgement, but for me it is not the moment when we watch passively how our verdict is announced.

> For me, Last Judgement is the moment when we finally stand in the presence of Christ and can choose to recognize him as the Lord of Love and Goodness or not.
>
> For me, it is the moment when we look back to our life together with Christ, in his presence, and either regret what went wrong in our lives and where we hurt people, or not.
>
> For me, it is the moment when the hate and anger, grief and greed which we all carry, can either fall off and leave us or continue to reign our heart and influence our whole being and character.

Last Judgement is a last choice given by Christ to repent and to turn to God as the only source of everlasting life, fully accepting God's justice and rule or to stay in our own self-made life concepts where we decide what is just or not, where we decide what is right or wrong, who is in or out according to our drawers of race, gender, wealth, sexuality, nationality, class, et cetera. According to that last choice, Christ will separate the sheep and the goats. Hell, I believe, is a self-chosen option, but more about this in the next section.

Heaven & Hell

Inspired by a number of Bible verses and then especially by visions of Saints like Bede or Boniface or the poet Dante and his *Commedia Divina*, images of fire, torture, several chambers with different intensity of torture and the idea of purgatory have kept people's fantasies busy and them afraid.

Purgatory

The teaching that something like Purgatory, a cleansing temporal pain in fire after death, existed was, originally, considered a grace.[1] The belief in Purgatory gave most people who knew that they would not be found completely blameless at the end of their life, hope. If they did not commit any of the deadly sins, they would not go to hell for eternal damnation, but serve a sentence of a certain time in the pain of a cleansing fire and after that sentence had been served, they would be allowed entrance into heaven. So life was about keeping the time in this fire as short as possible, or—the fundraising idea of the church in the sixteenth century—you bought your way out of Purgatory.

If we forget about Purgatory as a place of real fire, where the soul spends years and from where you can buy a ticket to freedom by money, then it makes sense that we need to go through a process of cleansing and purification before we enter into heaven, a sphere of complete justice and God's light. If we entered like we are, heaven would be nothing else but another earth with the same human-made issues.

Linked to the image drawn about the Last Judgement above, I believe in Purgatory to be a cleansing moment in the presence of Christ. Imagine you find yourself in Christ's presence, who is the ultimate goodness, justice, love. In his presence, you realize what real justice, what real love actually is and you start to see clearly what God's plan for this creation looks like. With this new enlightenment, Christ makes you look back to your life and the *Book of Life* brings up moments from your life like scenes from a movie and you watch yourself acting, now looking through the lenses of God. Suddenly, we would become aware of the consequences of our actions. Suddenly, we would see what a quick harsh word

1. Already the Church Fathers Irenaeus and Clement of Alexandria followed by Origen believed in purification after death.

to someone stirred up in that person, we would see the pain our behavior has caused for people, we would see the hidden consequences of our actions and behavior. I do not think shame would be the only feeling coming up in me; I am sure I will be in pain on that day to see how often and how badly I have and will have failed against my siblings in Christ during the time I wandered on this earth. This pain of being sorry, this shame, this despair facing the fact that it will be too late in that moment to heal or to seek forgiveness, this pain will be like torture, it will be like a fire burning inside. This is, what I believe to be the cleansing fire of Purgatory. When we finished the review of our life, we will know fully who we are and how much we depend and have always depended on the boundless grace and mercy of God. We will be ready to start again, a new life in the full presence of goodness. We will be able to live what we are already called to be right now: a new creation.

Eternal damnation

How can it be then that the Bible speaks about eternal damnation or the fire that does not cleanse but burn? Is there a place of fire where some people will spend eternity? We do not have to think long, to come up with people in history or present time who are so much driven by hatred, by sinfulness, by destructive concepts or Weltanschauungen[2] and have internalized these harmful doctrines through and through that it is easy to think that they would not see the evil that reigns them, even in the presence of God. I could imagine that it is people like these who will fail in the cleansing fire because they do not see what they need cleansing from. But what happens with them? The Bible gives us an example of such a person and of their fate.

For years, the rich man lived in his house in pure luxury. He celebrated parties, ate a lot, drank the best wines and never had to worry about money. For years, this rich man had to pass poor Lazarus who slept on the street before the rich man's house. He

---

2. German for the plural of "worldview."

always looked the other direction when he passed him because he did not like to see the dirty clothes and the hungry eyes. After a big party, the servants of the rich man brought the food waste, what was left on the plates, out and Lazarus could eat from it, if the dogs were not faster. For the rich man, that was the natural order of the world: the rich live in luxury and enjoy their privileges and the poor are there to serve the rich and else to get out of their way. The story told in Luke is no Hollywood drama with a nice happy end. There is no justice for Lazarus as long as he lives. In the story Lazarus dies as the poor man he had been most or all of his life and the rich man dies rich and having his luxuries at hand to the very last moment. What is important is what happens then.

Lazarus is taken up by angels and brought into the care of God (the story says into the care of *father Abraham*). Lazarus finds himself in a happy place, in good care and he finds love which had been denied to him all his life.

The rich man finds himself in a state of pain. He suffers. The pain of hell? Interestingly, he can see Lazarus sitting next to Abraham. This means that there is still a connection, they are in one sphere, but one is happy and the other consumed by pain. The rich man can even communicate with them. He calls to them saying that he is so hot and thirsty:

> "Father Abraham, have mercy on me, and send Lazarus
> to dip the tip of his finger in water and cool my tongue"
> (Luke 16:24a).

Lazarus did not come to serve him water and he continued to suffer. How does this story go together with the concept of Last Judgement and the idea that hell and eternal damnation are self-chosen? When the rich man died, I believe he—like everyone—came before Christ, the judge, and in his presence reviewed his life. In the presence of Christ, he saw how much Lazarus suffered while he was enjoying himself beyond measure and he saw that he had the means to make a significant change in Lazarus's life. The rich man, however, did not feel that he had acted wrongly. Even in the presence of the pure and unconditional love of God, he did not see a problem in his behavior and in the fate of Lazarus. He did not feel the pain every other human would feel in that moment—nor the wish to repent. He did not go through the cleansing fire and feel the pain of regret and sorrow in the face of his own wrongdoings and the harm he had caused. Consequently, he condemned himself to eternal pain. For eternity, he will be completely convinced that it is the natural position of the poor to serve the rich. For eternity, he will believe that it is right and fair that the rich have all the privileges in the world while the poor suffer and hunger for food and justice. For eternity, he will see the complete opposite happening in the Kingdom of God: he has to endure the fact that the poor (who should serve the rich), sit in a place of honor next to God and do not serve him when he calls. He sees his deepest conviction denied and it causes him pain, deep burning pain.[3]

This is, I believe, eternal damnation and suffering in hell. It is for people who, even after death and after having encountered the presence of God, do not drop their concepts of hatred, superiority, class, racism and believe that their idea of justice should also rule in heaven. Think of dictators and warlords who fight for their privileges, who fight for the superiority of one race or whatever principles, and, then, in the Kingdom of God they suddenly see the ones they have oppressed or killed their whole lives sitting in places of honor. It will torture them worse than fire: Heaven will feel like Hell for them.

Satan

After this concept of Hell has been presented, a question remains: where and how does the devil/Satan play into this?

The foundations for this question have been laid in the chapter about Theodicy, the question how there can be suffering in the world. The question about the existence of the devil or Satan is the question about the source of evil in the world. Has God created

---

3. This interpretation of Luke 16 has been strongly inspired by Rob Bell's *Love Wins*.

evil as its own entity (being/existence), does evil act according to God's commands, does evil have an independent source apart from God or is evil a by-product of freedom?

The Bible uses all kinds of ways to talk about evil and evil forces. Very often, we find evil personified as dark or fallen angels, as a person (Satan in the desert with Jesus), as an invisible and abstract power (as in the Parable of the sower who also sows on the paths where "the evil one comes and snatches away what is sown," Mtt 13:19b).

A very influential belief has been the idea that Satan was originally an angel of God in heaven, who then turned away from God and became evil. In the Book of Job, God even strikes bargains with Satan. Athanasius of Alexandria makes the interesting point that, actually, evil does not really exist.[4] He argues that everything in this world only exists because God created it and he would ask: how could God, who is pure goodness, have created something bad? Where should the bad come from when the source is goodness? He does not say, he cannot see evil in the world but he would argue that the evil we experience is a human-made concept. It was neither in the nature of this world or of humans or of creation as a whole but humans invented the concept and started acting according to it. This is an interesting point. The up-side of it: God is out of the cross-examination because God created everything well. It also has a positive concept of humans, who have been created as good and only later corrupted their own goodness by decision. It cannot explain disaster and pain which is not human-made. The concept also does not mention the tradition of personified evil.

As mentioned in the chapter on Theodicy, I cannot easily excuse God. The possibility that God holds good and evil and lets good and evil happen in the world, cannot easily be pushed aside and remains open for me.

What helps me with the question of personified evil is the story of Jesus and the Tempter (devil/Satan) in the desert, when Satan tempts Jesus (Mtt 4). This story was used in the chapter about

---

4. Athanasius, *Contra Gentes*, 1–8, especially 2.1; 4.18; 7.15.

sin. It is the story about the Tempter appearing to Jesus after Jesus had been fasting for forty days, and then starts to tempt Jesus.

> "If you are the Son of God, command these stones to become loaves of bread (Mtt 4:3b).
>
> If you are the Son of God, throw yourself down [from the pinnacle of the temple]; for it is written . . . " (and what follows is a quote from Psalm 91 about the angels of God saving the believer; Mtt 4:6b).
>
> "All these [lands] I will give you, if you will fall down and worship me" (Mtt 4:9b).

Maybe this story uses a personification for something most of us have experienced: the other voice within us. Perhaps the Tempter is meant to be this disturbing and often up-setting and off-putting voice that throws unwelcome thoughts into the constant flow of our other thoughts; this voice that suddenly repeats racist arguments which we personally despise, that says something horrible about a person next to us, that wants to encourage us to feel superior to someone.

Maybe that is the real devil/tempter/Satan: it is that voice within us that brings evil thoughts to our minds even though we do not want to have them and are sometimes embarrassed in front of ourselves that such a thought came up. This voice is the evil and it can become real when we give in to that voice and listen to it instead of fighting it back and arguing against it. St. Paul knew that voice:

> "I do not understand my own actions. For I do not do what I want, but I do the very thing I hate . . . I can will what is right, but I cannot do it. For I do not do the good I want, but the evil I do not want is what I do. Now, if I do what I do not want, it is no longer I that do it, but sin that dwells within me" (Rom 7:15, 19–20).

In the moment we let this voice win the inner argument, evil becomes manifest in the world and we will act on advice of this evil voice: Satan is born. Athanasius was right: evil does not exist on its own; it is a human concept that can manifest itself in the world when we give our hands, our feet and our service to it.

Second Coming

Among the early Christians, the main hope for a Christian was not so much the perspective of going to heaven and being united with God one day; it was rather the strong belief that the Second Coming of Christ to this earth was imminent. People hoped that Christ would come again and put affairs into order here on this earth, in our lives; right what is wrong, and bring justice where there is injustice. Then we would see what comes after but the first hope was the coming of Christ as promised so often in Scripture: "This Jesus, who has been taken up from you into heaven, will come in the same way as you saw him go into heaven" (Acts 1:11b).

Jesus himself seemed to have expected his return and the coming of the Kingdom of God sooner. His message was: "The Kingdom of God is at hand" (Mark 1:15b). It is right that, as Christians, we believe that the Kingdom of God has begun in Jesus's ministry, in his healing, in the presence of God in him. However, the Kingdom of God has not yet been fulfilled. We still see injustice, pain, war, greed and all the other imperfections in the world. As Christians, we wait for Christ to return and to bring the earth and all its life in line with the original intention of God in Creation.

It is interesting that the focus on the Second Coming has shifted over time. In the Middle Ages in Central Europe, the afterlife came more and more into focus. The reasons for this were more complex than the simple concept that life in the Middle Ages was so hard that the only hope was for a better life after death. In the late Middle Ages, people were more and more unsure whether they were on the saved side and people were massively concerned with questions around purgatory and hell and how to enhance their chances to get into heaven. This is, of course, simplifying very complex developments in spirituality and faith across geographic and cultural boundaries but I hope it helps a bit to get some big lines of shifts in Christian spirituality. Another shift was definitely the Reformation and following the Early Modern period. Life on earth became one long-stretched new focus. Even though Karl Marx was still very upset with Christianity's focus on after-life instead of trying to improve life on earth, compared to earlier periods, the *Now* became more and more important and with it, Christianity developed its strong code of ethics. We, today, are coming out of a period when the main focus was on ethical behavior as the main Christian message and we find ourselves in a period when the focus is beginning to recalibrate itself.

I believe that we should widen our focus again so that being Christian is not the same thing as just subscribing to some kind of ethical moral code. Today, we need the power which is held by the hope that death is not the end but a door to a world where God's rule is unquestioned and where everyone is really equal and loved. But today does also need the strong call to action, neither just to be nice to everyone and wait until life is over, nor to have the only focus on the after-life when everything will be better. No, today, we also need the call to prepare this earth for the coming of the Kingdom of God. This is our task as Christians in the world: we cannot bring the Kingdom of God about, but we have to prepare its way. It is our vocation to make this earth a better place and prepare our hearts and the hearts of others for the full unfolding of the Love of God. The Kingdom will not happen in a world where people do not care that other humans are mistreated, are hungry, poor. The Kingdom will not come fully as long as the world is indifferent to the suffering of other humans, to the destruction of creation and its creatures. We need to hear the wake-up call and we need to be the multipliers and advocates of God and prepare this world for the Second Coming.

The Second Coming of Christ has nothing in it that allows us to lean back and think that everything will be fine in the end anyway. The Second Coming is the kick we lazy Christians need to live in the world what we say on a Sunday and what we hopefully belief in our hearts.

VIII

Quod erat demonstrandum

QUOD ERAT DEMONSTRANDUM: WHAT was to be shown. This book did not intend to give nicely packaged answers to the big questions of faith; it wants to be a companion on the way to inspire people to think, pray, meditate and to find their own answers and develop their own Dishwasher Theology. Theology is about life-long learning and listening. No answer we find will ever remain the same and the *best* theologian will be quite surprised on the day when we stand face to face with our maker.

If you take one thing from this small book, then, I hope, it is the encouragement to think for yourself and to remain open for whatever insights and new understandings God is granting you. It is all about a faithful, prayerful growing and walking in faith.

When you come to believe something, always ask yourself: where is the Good News in this? If you cannot find the Good News, search harder and if you can still not find any, then it might not be from God.

Be Blessed on your path.

About the Author

André (pronouns: he/him/his) is of German origin and was born in the Black Forest in 1989. After he spent most of his teenage years dreaming of and working for a political career, he discovered the church as a place of community and spiritual growth. He became a member of Parish Council in the German Protestant parish in his home town and graduated from school. From early on, he got to know the Anglican Church and grew spiritually with one leg in the Protestant Church and one in the Anglican Church.

His university career brought him around the world. First studying History and English, he discovered over the years that there is no way to run from a vocation to ordained ministry which made him take on theology as his main subject. His academic education led him to Konstanz and Freiburg (Germany), Durham (UK), Basel (Switzerland), Jerusalem where he studied two semesters at Dormition Abbey (a German Benedictine Monastery on Mt. Sion) and served at St. George's Anglican Cathedral and to Westcott House, Cambridge (UK).

He served as Curate at Basel Cathedral and was ordained into the Swiss Reformed Church before a call brought him to the Diocese of New Westminster, where he was ordained Deacon and Priest at Christ Church Cathedral, Vancouver. André served his Anglican Curacy at Christ Church Cathedral before serving as Rector of St. Clement Anglican Church, North Vancouver, in the Diocese of New Westminster. André feels fully at home in both church traditions—the Anglican and the Protestant/Reformed—and the ecumenical dialogue is a passion of his.

Today, he works as Research Assistant at Bern University.

Sources & References

Anglican Church of Canada, *The Book Of Common Prayer and Administration of the Sacraments and Other Rites and Ceremonies of the Church According to the Use of the Anglican Church of Canada: Together with the Psalter.* Toronto: Anglican Book Centre, 1962.

Anselm of Canterbury, *The Major Works.* Edited by Brian Davies and G. R. Evans. Oxford: Oxford University Press, 1998.

————. *Opera omnia.* Edited by Franciscus Salesius Schmitt. 6 Volumes. Edinburgh: Thomas Nelson, 1938.

————. "Why God Became Man." In *The Major Works*, edited by Brian Davies and G. R. Evans, 260-356. Oxford: Oxford University Press, 1998.

Athanasius, *Contra Gentes and De Incarnatione.* Edited and translated by Robert W. Thomson. Oxford Early Christian Texts. Oxford: Oxford University Press, 1971.

Barth, Karl, *Nein! Antwort an Emil Brunner.* München: Christian Kaiser, 1934.

Bell, Rob, *Love wins: At the Heart of Life's Big Questions.* New York: Collins, 2012.

Diangelo, Robin, *White Fragility: Why it's so Hard for White People to Talk about Racism.* Boston: Beacon, 2018.

Gaius Suetonius Tranquillus, *The Twelve Caesars.* Translated by Robert Graves. 1957, revised by James B. Rives. Harmondsworth: Penguin, 2007.

Martin Luther, *D Martin Luther's Werke.* Kritische Gesamtausgabe (WA DB). 120 volumes. Weimar: Hermann Böhlau, 1883–2009.

Moltmann, Jürgen, *Der Gekreuzigte Gott. Das Kreuz Christi als Grund und Kritik Christlicher Theologie.* München: Christian Kaiser, 1972.

www.ingramcontent.com/pod-product-compliance
Lightning Source LLC
LaVergne TN
LVHW021617080426
835510LV00019B/2628